GARLAND STUDIES IN

ENTREPRENEURSHIP

T0347649

edited by
STUART BRUCHEY
ALLAN NEVINS PROFESSOR EMERITUS
COLUMBIA UNIVERSITY

GENDERED CAPITAL

ENTREPRENEURIAL WOMEN IN AMERICAN SOCIETY

SALLY ANN DAVIES-NETZLEY

Routledge
Taylor & Francis Group
New York   London

First published 2000 by Garland Publishing, Inc.

This edition published 2013 by Routledge
711 Third Avenue, New York, NY 10017
2 Park Square, Milton Park, Abingdon, Oxfordshire OX14 4RN

First issued in paperback 2014

Routledge is an imprint of the Taylor & Francis Group, an informa business

Library of Congress Cataloging-in-Publication Data
Davies-Netzley, Sally Ann.
     Gendered capital : entrepreneurial women in American society / Sally Ann
Davies-Netzley.
          p. cm. — (Garland studies in entrepreneurship)
     Includes bibliographical references and index.
     ISBN 0-8153-3869-4 (alk. paper)
     1. Self-employed women—California—San Diego County—Case studies.
     2. Businesswomen—California—San Diego County—Case studies.
     3. Entrepreneurship—California—San Diego County—Case studies. I. Title.
     II. Series.
     HD6072.6.U5 D38 2000
     305.43'338'09794985—dc21   00-034729

ISBN 13: 978-1-138-86556-3 (pbk)
ISBN 13: 978-0-8153-3869-7 (hbk)

For Steve

Contents

Preface and Acknowledgments

Gendered Capital arose out of my interest in women's work-related trends. I was especially taken by the fact that women in the United States have started businesses at twice the rate of men in recent years. Today women in the United States are involved in the ownership of many different kinds of business enterprises. Some own home-based sole proprietorships. Others have established large corporations with employees. Why have women increasingly been turning to business ownership? How might race and ethnicity impact women's entrepreneurship? *Gendered Capital* compares the experiences of 89 white and Latina women entrepreneurs who own and operate businesses in San Diego County. The book explores the various pathways that women take to becoming entrepreneurs in American society and examines the economic, social, and cultural capital they use along the way.

The first two chapters introduce the research, study methods, and sample. I used a variety of sources for initial interviews, including the Small Business Administration in San Diego, the San Diego County Minority Women Enterprise directory, and Chamber of Commerce business lists. I selected most of the participants from the San Diego County directory of fictitious business names.

Chapter 3 explores five main reasons why women become entrepreneurs, including family-related concerns, wanting freedom from corporate bureaucracy, being laid off from previous employment, reacting to gender discrimination in prior workplaces, and having the right opportunity. Chapter 4 examines the capital of women entrepreneurs. Most often, the literature on entrepreneurship associates capital with financial resources. This study expands on that notion by incorporating Pierre Bourdieu's framework of three forms of capital: economic, social, and cultural. I discuss women entrepreneurs" economic capital in the form of savings, credit cards, family sources, and formal lending institutions. I also reveal the nature of women's social capital, where they turn to for business advice and assistance, including mentors and family. This is followed by discussion of the cultural resources that women feel are necessary to succeed as business owners. Chapter 5 is devoted entirely to Latina women in order to explore their unique issues as women minority entrepreneurs. In the conclusion, I elaborate on the women's future goals and discuss directions for future research.

The women portrayed in this book are in a wide array of industries, from biotechnology to floral design. Their gross receipts and sales vary considerably. Yet they share much. They find fulfillment in business ownership. They value the control, freedom, and flexibility that comes from being your own boss.

I wish to thank the 89 women entrepreneurs who are profiled in this book. Without their time and assistance, I would not have been able to carry out this study.

Thanks to Garland Publishing for publishing this book and allowing my work to reach a much wider audience than it would have. Many thanks to my doctorate dissertation advisors, Professors Judith Stepan-Norris, Leo Chavez, and Judith Treas, at the University of California Irvine. I especially appreciate their feedback on this research, from early proposals to later drafts. They have taught me how to become a better scholar and writer. I would also like to acknowledge the Center for Research on Latinos in a Global Society and the Social Relations Graduate Studies Committee at the University of California Irvine for financial support with this study.

Many thanks also to my parents, sister, and grandparents for their love and support. Last, but most importantly, I dedicate this book with love to my husband, Steve.

Gendered Capital

CHAPTER 1

First Encounters

When I first called Patty Rogers' accounting business to set up an interview, a polite, rather timid voice answered the phone. I explained the purpose of my call. I was conducting social science research on women business owners and wished to speak with Patty. Within minutes, Patty picked up the line and agreed to meet with me the following week. It wasn't apparent to me that Patty's business was home based until she gave me directions to the residential address where her office was located.

The day of the interview was dry and uncomfortably hot, over ninety degrees. Patty's home-based business is located in a quiet, suburban area of East County San Diego, about half an hour from downtown and a substantial drive from North County, the areas in which most San Diegans work. The scenery becomes decidedly more rural and desert-like the further ones travels east.

When I pulled up the steep gravel driveway to Patty's home, I was greeted by two black Scottish terriers, dusty from lying in the landscaping. They excitedly ran around the car as I parked. Then, a man driving a Honda Civic pulled up. We exchanged "good afternoons" and I mentioned that I was there to see Patty. We walked up to the front door and rang the bell several times before someone answered. The door was eventually opened by a woman, twentysomething, dressed in jeans and a white t-shirt. A shrill voice then echoed up the stairs, "Stan, is that you?" "Yes," the man next to me replied. "Come down here and let's get that return sorted out," the voice responded. Stan and the young woman went down the staircase while I waited in the entry way. The voice shouted again, "Sally, I'll be right up."

From the entry way I could see the kitchen, dining room, formal living room, and family room. The house was relatively dark. A few rays of sunlight peeked through the sides of some wooden blinds, closed in an attempt to keep out the heat. Standing there, I was struck by the number of children's toys throughout the house—*When I Was Five* and other children's books on the living room table, "I Squeak" stuffed animals on the floor, and a multicolor, Playschool plastic jungle gym in the family room. Family and school photos hung in the formal living room. Blue crayon marks, about three feet high, decorated the family room walls. Laundry was heaped on the living room sofa.

I could overhear voices downstairs. "Stan you look much better. When I saw you last I didn't think you'd make it more than a week. But you look like you're doing much better." Stan responded with a comment about successful cancer treatment, and the conversation apparently turned to his tax return extension. About five minutes later, a woman in her early 40s wearing shorts and a t-shirt made her way up the stairs. She introduced herself as Patty.

Patty escorted me to her office space—the downstairs level of her home. Two rooms had been converted into offices with desks, computers, and file cabinets. Accounting documents were interspersed among crayon drawn pictures and family photos. In Patty's office, a pile of toys sat a foot high at the base of an open closet. Patty explained that she was in the middle of cleaning out the closet and that the office was not usually so messy. She emphasized that while some clients, like Stan, drop by, most often she goes out to clients' businesses or does business over the phone or through mail and fax.

Patty begins the interview by raving about the obvious advantages of having a home-based business with three young children. She and her husband, Frank, have a nine, five, and two year old. "If I am working here, I can be in my pajamas, my kids can be upstairs sleeping and I don't need a babysitter. I know they are safe because I know they are just upstairs."

I ask Patty about her decision to establish a business of her own. She explains that her entrepreneurial spirit was fueled by her mother who, after her husband passed away, supported the family by engaging in a number of small business ventures.

> My mom started her own business and worked an average of 70 hours a week for years and years to see us through. Her business was driving a route of specialty cleaning. She cleaned pillows, feathered pillows, leather, and other things that are hard to clean. She would drive to L.A. and Orange County to specialty cleaning houses.

Patty is thankful for her mother's hard work, which enabled her and her three siblings to make it through childhood still having a roof over their heads in a safe neighborhood, plenty of food, and even new clothes at the beginning of most school years. After graduating from high school and earning a bachelors degree in business administration, Patty found a job in accounting. In order to gain a more lucrative position, Patty decided to return to university. She finished her MBA in the early 1980s. By this time, she was married to Frank, who was a security guard at the university she had attended. Patty began working for one of the "Big Eight" upon graduation.

> I was at [the company] for five years. The last year I was there I had my son. So I had my son and took maternity leave. And when I called to say I would be back, they said, "Oh, we didn't think you would be coming back so we gave your clients away and we really don't need you for a few months." I said, "Okay." You know, it was okay, financially, we could do that.... [When I came back] I was traveling all over the country for [the company], and my son traveled with me everywhere and I nursed him and I would go to work and I would come back at lunch and nurse and then at dinner, I would take him down to the restaurant and we would eat and visit and have our fun and he would go to bed in my hotel room. We did that for a year.

Patty soon tired of the demanding travel schedule and work hours of a senior accountant and decided to take a lower-paying job at a smaller firm. After two years on the job, Patty explains, "They did a complete reorganization. They wanted me to know that, "You had done a great job for us for two years, so we are not letting you go, but your position no longer exists."" Patty was laid off. Her next career move involved working as an accounting consultant for several small, local businesses. Through these initial contacts, Patty finally established her own accounting business as a sole proprietorship in 1994.

> My business now has been good. I have over 35 business clients and I meet with them. Most I have gotten from referrals or as referrals. Sometimes I advertise locally in the church bulletin and the Chamber of Commerce and local newspaper...There is one women's group I go to. The referrals are only a $150 tax return or a $300 tax return but once I do them, then I do auntie May and cousin George and so there is plenty of that.

But it took more than making contacts and referrals to get her business going. In addition to social connections, Patty needed economic capital. Frank's salary as a security guard offered a stable income to support their three children, but could not generate the savings Patty needed to establish the business. She turned to her mother for the financial resources necessary to start her business.

> I have had a fairly easy source for myself, borrowed from my mom and had to pay her back at a fair market rate, whatever. Over the years, over the last three years, I have had maybe a total of $12,000, you know $2,000 or $3,000 a time during the turnaround, from my mother. My mom stuck her money in the credit union at you know 3 percent and I will give her 8 or something, and I

can't get that at a bank and there are no credit card fees, you know. So I
actually owe her at this point less than $1,000, so but I mean she helped me
pay for my first computers three years ago.

Depending on the time of year, Patty works between 40 and 80 hours per
week at her business. She also has one full-time assistant, the young woman who
greeted me at the door. Her business grosses about $80,000 in receipts annually,
a number that steadily diminishes into a net estimate of $25,000 to $30,000.
Patty's plans for the future include eventually moving into an office building
when her children are older, and possibly hiring her husband full-time when he
retires from security work.[1]

Patty Rogers has joined the millions of women in this country who have
established their own businesses. Women in the United States have owned
businesses since the colonial period, most as silent partners or unpaid workers in
family-owned businesses (Bird 1976). But today women are involved more
directly in the labor force as paid workers and more visibly in the ownership of
businesses. The number of women-owned businesses has dramatically increased
in recent years.

Such a trend offers added significance to the questions posed in this book.
Who are these new women entrepreneurs in American society? In an economy
that is dominated by wage and salary employees, why are women increasingly
choosing to enter business for themselves? What forms of capital do they use to
succeed as entrepreneurs? These questions form the basis of this study on
women's entrepreneurship.

WOMEN IN THE U.S. LABOR FORCE

Any discussion of women's entrepreneurship in the United States should be
placed within the larger, historical context of women's work patterns. In
preindustrial, colonial America, women often performed household duties such
as cooking, cleaning, and child care. In addition, they provided goods for the
colonial economy by spinning thread, weaving cloth, and making soap, shoes,
and candles (Blau and Winkler 1989). Women also engaged in a range of
business activities like working as tavern keepers, store managers, traders,
printers, seamstresses, tailors, and domestic servants (Blau and Winkler 1989).

With the rise of industrialization, the ideological split between publicly
organized production and privately organized consumption and reproduction
was given concrete form in the doctrine of separate spheres (Glenn 1994). This
doctrine posited that men's place was in the public sphere of the economy, while
women and children belonged in the private sphere of the household. Women
were viewed as responsible for home work and men were viewed as
breadwinners responsible for market work (Blau and Winkler 1989). Juliet

Mitchell (1998) argues that social coercion, rather than women's physical deficiency, has prompted the gender division of labor. "Women have been forced to do "women's work." Of course, this force may not be actualized as direct aggression" (Mitchell 1998:176). Instead, Mitchell (1998) argues, coercion has been "ameliorated to an ideology shared by both sexes" (p. 178).

At the turn of the twentieth century, a small percent of married women had jobs outside the home, but this pattern did not prevail among all groups of women. Many women—poor and working class, immigrants, racial and ethnic minorities—often combined income earning in and out of the home with child care and domestic labor (Glenn 1994). African American women, many of whom still resided in the South, and immigrant women in Northern, textile-manufacturing towns were two major groups of married women for whom work outside the home was quite common (Blau and Winkler 1989).

Since the beginning of the century, women's increased labor force participation in the United States stands out as a significant trend. In 1900, women's labor force participation rate was 20 percent in the United States (Gerson 1985). In the early decades of the twentieth century, white middle class women were often employed in "new" white collar fields, such as clerical work, while white working class and ethnic minority women tended to work in factories (Anderson 1988). Many immigrant women often worked as domestics in other people's homes (Pedraza 1991). During this time, male workers resisted the entrance of women and children into the industrial labor force by excluding them from union membership and pushing for protective labor laws for women and children (Hartmann 1981). Hartmann (1981) explains that male workers "argued for wages sufficient for their wage labor alone to support their families. . . . Instead of fighting for equal wages for men and women, male workers sought the family wage, wanting to retain their wives' services at home" (p. 21). According to Hartmann (1981), because capitalists realized that housewives produced healthier workers than wage-working wives, paying family wages to men and keeping women at home suited capitalists and male workers at that time. Hartmann (1981) argues that the family wage is still the cornerstone of the present gender division of labor in which men are primarily responsible for wage work and women primarily for housework.

The influx of women into the labor force increased during the 1940s due to labor shortages resulting from the mobilization of men to fight in World War II (U.S. Department of Labor 1995a). In 1940, the labor force included 28 percent of the female population age 14 and over (Blau and Winkler 1989). Between 1940 and 1945, the female labor force grew by over 5 million; 36 percent of all women age 14 and over were in the labor force in 1945 (Blau and Winkler 1989). Women were often displaced from jobs in the immediate postwar period as the cult of female domesticity reached its height (Rubin 1994). The postwar expansion created favorable conditions for many Americans to buy homes on the strength of the husband's income alone and have families tended by mothers who could afford to stay home. Still, women's labor force participation continued to rise as the U.S. economy experienced a boom in service-producing industries like health, education, and banking.

By the late 1970s almost half of all women 14 years of age and over were in the labor force (Blau and Winkler 1989). During the past several decades, wage stagnation and periodic economic recessions have squeezed family income and prompted more women into the labor force. In 1970, 30 percent of married women with children under age 6 worked outside the home; by 1991, 60 percent of these women were in the labor force (Rubin 1994). While the American economy saw an expansion in high technology and services in the 1980s, growth in blue-collar factory, transportation, and construction jobs, traditionally held by men, has not kept pace with the working-age population (Wilson 1996). As a result, these men are working less while women continue to move into jobs in the expanding social service sector.

Currently, nearly six in 10 women over age 16 participate in the U.S. work force (U.S. Department of Labor 1996). Women now account for 46 percent of the total United States labor force participants and are projected to comprise 48 percent by the year 2005 (U.S. Department of Labor 1996). Women's labor force participation continues to vary by marital status. Divorced women have higher participation rates (74 percent) than married women (61 percent) or never married women (66 percent) (U.S. Department of Labor 1996).

Women's contemporary increases in labor force participation have resulted from a combination of factors, including economic shifts, changing views about women's roles, women's higher educational attainment and expanded opportunities for career advancement, rising divorce rates, and increasing numbers of single parent households. Increased access to income through labor market participation has resulted in contradictory outcomes for women. For many dual-income families, a paycheck can mean women's increased independence and decision-making in the home. And for many female-headed and poor households, like Patty Rogers' childhood home, women's paid work translates into family survival. But the price paid for access to these economic resources is competing in a race and gender segregated labor market. Women's activities within the private household sphere and their roles in wage employment continue to be shaped by the gender division of labor and its ideology defining the household as women's primary responsibility (Rapp 1982, Tiano 1994).

Table 1.1 Employed Persons by Occupation and Sex, 1974 and 1994 Annual Averages

Occupation	Men		Women	
	1974	1994	1974	1994
Total Employed (Thousands)	53 024	66 450	33 769	56 610
Percent Distribution				
Managerial, Professional	**22. 0**	**26. 5**	**17. 6**	**28. 7**
Executive, Administrative, Managerial	12. 1	14. 0	5. 0	12. 4
Professional Specialty	9. 9	12. 5	12. 6	16. 3
Technical, Sales, Administrative Support	**18. 5**	**20. 0**	**45. 1**	**42. 4**
Technicians, Related	2. 4	2. 8	2. 5	3. 6
Sales	10. 1	11. 4	11. 0	12. 8
Administrative Support	6. 0	5. 9	31. 6	26. 0
Service Occupations	**8. 1**	**10. 3**	**20. 6**	**17. 8**
Private Household	. 1	(¹)	3. 6	1. 4
Protective Service	2. 3	2. 8	. 3	. 7
Other Service	5. 8	7. 4	16. 8	15. 7
Precision Production, Craft, Repair	**19. 7**	**18. 4**	**1. 8**	**2. 2**
Operators, Fabricators, Laborers	**25. 4**	**20. 4**	**13. 3**	**7. 7**
Machine Operators, Assemblers Inspectors	10. 4	7. 2	10. 3	5. 2
Transportation, Material Move	7. 6	7. 0	. 6	. 9
Handlers, Equipment Cleaners, Helpers, Laborers	7. 4	6. 1	2. 4	1. 6
Farming, Fishing, Forestry	**6. 4**	**4. 4**	**1. 6**	**1. 2**

¹ Less than 0.05 percent
Source: U.S. Department of Labor 1995a.

Even though more women have entered the work force, the kind of work men and women do remains largely distant. The gender division of labor reappears in the labor market, in which women often work at the very jobs they do at home—food preparation and service, cleaning, and caring for people. The shift from the production of goods to the provision of services brought an explosion of new service-oriented, white collar jobs which were deemed more appropriate for women. Women entered these lower-tier, service-producing occupations in large numbers, in addition to clerical and administrative support occupations. In 1994, the proportion of women working in technical, sales, and administrative positions far outnumbered that of men (42 and 20 percent, respectively) (U.S. Department of Labor 1995a). If we break this category down further, it becomes clear that most of these men held sales occupations, while most women clustered in administrative support positions, such as secretarial or clerical work. In fact, 97 percent of all receptionists and 99 percent of all secretaries are women (U.S. Department of Labor 1995b).

Women have made gains into managerial and professional occupations in the United States. In 1994, the proportion of all working women employed in executive, managerial, and professional positions was 29 percent, which exceeded the comparable figure for men (27 percent) (U.S. Department of Labor 1995a). Still, these census categories mask the fact that women tend to cluster near the bottom of the organizational and semi-professional hierarchies and have lower earnings, authority, and advancement potential compared to men. Further, even in occupations predominantly held by women, such as nursing, the higher the position, the more likely the job holder to be male (Williams 1992).

The question of why occupations are so differentiated by gender has been the subject of considerable debate. One explanation focuses on human capital factors, such as education, training, years of work experience, interests, and attitudes. Human capital theorists assert that women look for jobs that are less demanding because they expect the need for flexibility due to child rearing and other domestic responsibilities (Becker 1985; Mincer and Polachek 1978). According to human capital theorists, gender segregation in the labor market results from women's economically rational decisions to limit their investments in training and pursue certain occupations. Other explanations challenge human capital theory and focus on women's exclusion from many occupations, job discrimination, and employers' stereotyping as reasons for gender segregation (Reskin 1993).

The fact that women are segregated in lower-paying occupations and industries explains much of the reason why women have overall earnings about three-fourths that of men (U.S. Department of Labor 1995a). Some of the sex gap in pay also can be attributed to women's fewer years seniority, overall employment experiences, and the intermittancy of such experience (England 1992). Still, some pay differences between men and women can be explained by gender discrimination and the unequal treatment of women in the labor market (Beeghley 1996; England 1992; Reskin 1993). Such discrimination is manifested in various ways including the exclusion of women from occupations on direct grounds, such as military combat, or through informal barriers, like the "glass ceiling," that prevent women from obtaining high-level work positions.

Clearly, women's work experiences are not only affected by gender, but also by race and ethnicity. Women and men of color face additional constraints of racial discrimination and informal barriers to occupational advancement (Collins 1989; Higginbotham 1994; Segura 1986). Jones (1985) details the history of employment of African American women in the United States. She finds that in the early twentieth century, African American women clustered in low-pay factory or domestic servant jobs, as racist employers refused to hire them in clerical or sales positions. Historically, African American women seeking higher education also have been steered into lower-pay professions such as school teaching, nursing, social work, and library sciences, and have tended to serve the African American community (Higginbotham 1994). Today, minority women in the United States continue to be overrepresented in low-paid occupations and underrepresented in high-paying professional jobs (Tang and Smith 1996). While part of the explanation lies in educational differences between white women and women of color, research suggests that minority women, even with advanced degrees, still struggle with racial discrimination and informal barriers to occupational advancement (Higginbotham 1994). Higginbotham's (1994) research indicates that African American professional and managerial women continue to cluster in public sector employment at a much higher rate than their non-African American counterparts.

Women who do reach higher paying jobs, like corporate presidents or board of directors members, tend to be white women from middle to upper class backgrounds. Even when at the top of the corporate ladder, these women often continue to experience an old boys network that can hinder their success (Davies-Netzley 1998; Dye 1995; Moore 1988; Zweigenhaft 1987). My research on men and women in corporate positions above the glass ceiling reveals that while white men tend to promote the dominant ideology of individualism, underscoring the significance of individual effort and talent as explanations of corporate mobility and success, white women offer alternative perspectives by emphasizing the significance of social networks and peer similarities for succeeding in elite positions (Davies-Netzley 1998). The women presidents and CEOs in my study negotiate old boy networks through a number of strategies, including modifying speech and behavior in order to fit into the male-dominated corporate scene.

THE GROWTH OF WOMEN'S ENTREPRENEURSHIP

Women's increased representation in the work force has been termed the silent revolution. From 1974 to 1994, the number of women working for pay almost doubled (U.S. Department of Labor 1995a). Remarkably, during that same time period, the number of women-owned businesses increased by almost a factor of fifteen (U.S. Bureau of the Census 1996a, 1976). Women-owned businesses have more than doubled since 1982, and now represent about one-third of all firms in the United States (U.S. Bureau of the Census 1996a, 1986). As of 1996, there were nearly 8 million women-owned firms in the U.S. (including C corporations) employing over 18 million workers. The sheer number of women becoming entrepreneurs in recent years makes the topic significant.

Figure 1.1 Women-Owned Businesses as a Percentage of all U.S. Businesses, 1972–1992

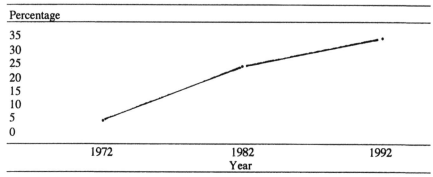

Source: U.S. Bureau of the Census, 1996a, 1986, 1976. Figure includes individual proprietorships,
partnerships, and subchapter S corporations. Excludes "C" corporations.

We can achieve further insight into women's entrepreneurial gains by taking a look at self-employment, a category in which most business owners fall. Over the last hundred years, there has been a notable decrease in the proportion of self-employed persons in the United States. C. Wright Mills (1951) argued that although the small capitalist once dominated the economic scene, this was no longer the case by 1950. "This is no society of small entrepreneurs," Mills (1951) asserted, "now they are one stratum among others: above them is the big money; below them, the alienated employee...behind them, their world" (p. 59). Today most entrepreneurs are self-employed. They establish sole proprietorships more often than corporations (in which they would be characterized as wage or salary workers). Estimates suggest that in the early nineteenth century about 80 percent of the U.S. labor force was self-employed. This proportion decreased to about 20 percent by 1940 (Mills 1951). This decrease in self-employment over time is mainly due to the industrialization of America and the reduction of agricultural employment and small farming in the United States (Bregger 1996).

After a long period of decline, self-employment began to show some signs of increasing in the United States during the mid 1970s. Current Population Surveys suggest that the self-employment rate climbed from 7.4 to 9.7 percent between 1975 and 1990 (Devine 1994).[2] This is still just half of what it was in 1940, but perhaps most noticeable about this contemporary trend is women's increased representation among the self-employed. In 1975, women represented about one-fourth of self-employed workers; women now comprise about one-third of the self-employed (Devine 1994). This change in the gender composition of the self-employed is, in part, reflected in differential changes in men's and women's employment rates—a 46 percent increase for women versus 24 percent for men from 1975 to 1990 (Devine 1994). However, women's self-employment rate increased by 63 percent during that same time period. From 1975 to 1990, women's self-employment rate climbed from 4.1 to 6.7 percent compared to 10 to 12.4 percent for men (Devine 1994).

Women's business ventures take place within a gender and race segregated labor market. Even as women establish themselves as small capitalists, the kinds of business ventures and industries they enter are potentially limited by gender ideologies. Like wage and salary women workers, women business owners continue to enter service and retail sectors at a higher rate than men. Many women-owned businesses are concentrated in the most "female" type fields, such as public relations, health, and beauty, and operate in low-growth industries or highly competitive markets (Loscocco and Robinson 1991).

WHY BECOME AN ENTREPRENEUR?

What prompts women in the United States to become entrepreneurs? Many classic sociological works on entrepreneurship neglect the concept of gender entirely (Parsons and Smelser 1956; Schumpeter 1934; Weber 1904–05/1958). The early literature examining gender and entrepreneurship in the United States emphasizes men's and women's personality traits and psychological determinants of entrepreneurship, while not accounting for significant social and economic factors, such as access to financial resources and social networking (Bender 1978; Schwartz 1976). More recent studies have focused on business problems encountered by women entrepreneurs (Hisrich and Brush 1984; Pellegrino and Reece 1982). Others determine the social and behavioral characteristics of women entrepreneurs (Fagenson 1993; Neider 1987), compare different generations of women entrepreneurs (Gregg 1985), or examine how women use corporate experience and contacts to establish their own businesses (Moore and Buttner 1997). Few of these studies, however, emphasize race and ethnicity or offer cross cultural comparisons.

There is a large body of literature on entrepreneurship among immigrants in the United States. It appears that "informal" entrepreneurial activities, such as under-the-table domestic work, are a route to entrepreneurship for many immigrant women who experience discrimination in formal-sector jobs or who enter the country as undocumented immigrants (Bonacich 1987; Chow 1994;

Glenn 1986; Hondagneu-Sotelo 1994; Safa 1981; Spalter-Roth 1988; Zhou 1992).

Scholars focusing on enterprises in the formal economy have developed several approaches for examining why ethnic minorities and immigrants create small-scale business enterprises in the United States. Some emphasize the significance of ethnic enclaves, labor market niches in which an available supply of ethnic labor and sources of capital sustain immigrant-owned businesses (Portes and Bach 1985). In such enclaves, ethnic or immigrant businesses, like Cuban-owned businesses in Miami, appear to rely on customers and workers of a common culture and background. Other scholars have developed a resource-based view of immigrant and ethnic entrepreneurship. Focusing on Korean entrepreneurship in Los Angeles, Light and Bonacich (1988) argue that Koreans' use of ethnic resources (social features of a group) and class resources (material assets, knowledge, and skills) have enabled the success of their small businesses. Further, Park's (1997) study of Korean immigrants in New York supports the segmented labor market model to explain Korean immigrant entrepreneurship. Park (1997) argues that Korean immigrants establish small businesses in response to their disadvantaged status in the American labor market. It is difficult for Korean immigrants to obtain good jobs due to cultural barriers and problems with untransferable skills and education (Park 1997). Park (1997) finds that most Korean businesses are male initiated, directed by the male household head. "Wives and other kin are expected to cooperate whatever way they can," Park argues (1997), "Whether they have professional training or not, women most commonly start to work in either factory jobs or as employees in small businesses, and later join their husband's businesses" (p. 116).

Many studies on ethnic and immigrant entrepreneurship neglect patterns of women-initiated formal business ownership. This book contributes to our understanding of gender and entrepreneurship by examining white and Latina women entrepreneurs who own and operate businesses in the formal U.S. economy. I compare these two groups of women entrepreneurs through data collected in San Diego County, in which the highest proportion of women-owned businesses are established by white and Latina women. My study includes women who have assisted in launching a business, accept its risks and responsibilities, and maintain involvement in its day-to-day functioning. This definition forms the basis of several other studies on women entrepreneurs (Lavoie 1984/1985; Moore and Buttner 1997). A further criteria of entrepreneurship in this study is that the women have a strong commitment to their businesses, which I define as being engaged with business activities full-time. This excludes women who view their businesses as part-time work or temporary ventures.

This book explores how women entrepreneurs' business ownership decisions emerge within American society and how women entrepreneurs strategically use capital to achieve their social and economic objectives. While accounting for the significance of gender and ethnicity, the book examines the various pathways that women take to becoming business owners. Is there a typical pathway to entrepreneurship for white and Latina women in the United States? The use of women's capital in their entrepreneurship is also assessed. How does women's access to different forms of capital shape these pathways?

THE IMPORTANCE OF CAPITAL

This book integrates Pierre Bourdieu's concepts of capital in order to better understand the resources available to women entrepreneurs and how they use these to meet their objectives. Bourdieu (1977) defines capital as "all the goods, material and symbolic, without distinction, that present themselves as rare and worthy of being sought after in a particular social formation" (p. 178). Bourdieu conceptualizes socially structured spaces in which agents struggle to either change or preserve the boundaries and form of these spaces. These agents compete for social positions by strategically employing economic, social, and cultural capital (Bourdieu 1984). This competition gives rise to social structure that positions agents according to the capital available to them (Bourdieu 1989). Bourdieu (1986) argues,

> The structure of the distribution of the different types and subtypes of capital at any given moment in time represents the immanent structure of the social world, i.e., the set of constraints, inscribed in the very reality of that world, which govern its functioning in a durable way, determining the chances of success for practices (p. 242).

Unlike the Marxian notion of class as a system based on property ownership, Bourdieu's concept of class takes into account three different forms of capital: economic, social, and cultural. For Bourdieu, the distribution of different social classes runs from those who are best provided with economic, social, and cultural capital, like professionals or senior executives, to those who are deprived in those respects (Bourdieu 1984). The distribution of different kinds of capital may also be asymmetrical, in the case of intellectuals or commercial employers, with cultural capital dominant in the former, and economic capital in the latter (Bourdieu 1984). Bourdieu (1986) argues that, ultimately, capital "is what makes the games of society—not least, the economic game—something other than simple games of chance" (p. 241).

Bourdieu's ideas have been applied to different physical and social locations, such as the educational system (Bourdieu and Passeron 1977;

Coleman 1988; Zweigenhaft 1993), the contemporary law firm (Granfield and Koenig 1992; Hagan et al 1991), and the urban ghetto (Fernandez-Kelly 1994). Researchers also use access to social capital to explain family economic well-being (Boisjoly et al 1995; Coleman 1988) and immigrant self-employment success (Sanders and Nee 1996).

Much of the literature on entrepreneurship focuses strictly on economic definitions of capital. Access to economic capital is crucial for women's business ownership start-up, development, and expansion. Acquiring adequate economic capital, especially from formal lending institutions, has tended to be a greater obstacle for women than men entrepreneurs (Bender 1978; Goffee and Scase 1985; Hisrich 1989; Hisrich and O'Brien 1981; Pelligrino and Reece 1982; Van der Wees and Romijn 1995). Women entrepreneurs may have difficulties in dealing with lending institutions because many lack financial track records in business or management (Hisrich 1989). Financial lenders may also discriminate against women-owned businesses because of gender ideologies marginalizing women's place in business (Marlow and Strange 1994). This book investigates how white and Latina women entrepreneurs obtain the start-up money for their businesses and who they turn to for these economic resources.

This exploration is intricately related to the forms of social capital available to the women. Social capital refers to valuable resources like social connections or networks of acquaintance, mutual trust, and recognition (Bourdieu 1984, 1986). Entrepreneurs are embedded in a social context, facilitated or inhibited by their position in social networks (Aldrich 1989; Granovetter 1985). Research suggests that minorities in the U.S., in particular African Americans and Latinos, are more likely than whites to rely on extended kinship networks for various social supports (Hays and Mindel 1973; Wagner and Schaffer 1980). In this book I examine how familialism relates to women's search for economic capital for new business ventures. I explore whether Latina women turn to family members for start-up capital more often than white women entrepreneurs.

Another significant concern relating to social capital involves who entrepreneurs turn to for business advice and assistance after having established their businesses. It is important to recognize that social networks used for business assistance are gendered and racialized. Research comparing men and women entrepreneurs finds that men entrepreneurs' advisor circles are mainly all-male, while women entrepreneurs are involved in mainly cross-sex networks with a high proportion of women (Aldrich and Sakano 1998). Social networks can be characterized by the strength of their ties. Strong-tie networks represent links with relatives or close friends that are usually of long duration and based on frequent contact. Weak-tie relationships involve acquaintances, are less reliable, of shorter duration, and involve lower frequency of contact (Granovetter 1985). Women appear to be left out of the informal weak-tie professional and business networks that provide men entrepreneurs access to diverse economic and cultural resources needed for business survival (Aldrich et al. 1989). When women entrepreneurs seek out business advice and assistance, they turn to women rather than men (Aldrich et al. 1995). In this book, I examine who women entrepreneurs ask for business advice and assistance and whether they feel isolated from all-male business networks.

While often ignoring gender, research on ethnic entrepreneurship in the United States indicates that co-ethnic social networks, such as protected ethnic markets and loyal co-ethnic employees, are often crucial for business success among some ethnic minorities and immigrants (Bonacich 1993; Light and Bonacich 1988; Portes and Bach 1985; Waldinger 1986). Immigrant entrepreneurs tend to run small businesses and rely on self-employment or unpaid family labor (Light and Bonacich 1988). A recent study by Dallalfar (1994) incorporates ethnicity and women's entrepreneurship, illustrating how Iranian immigrant women capitalize on shared customs in order to establish rapport with co-ethnic customers and use gender ideologies to legitimate businesses in the home, an environment viewed traditionally among Iranians as the special responsibility of women (Dallalfar 1994). My book asks: Is this also the case with immigrant and American-born Latina women business owners? Do they rely on co-ethnic networks and shared cultural ideals in order to succeed as entrepreneurs?

Accumulation of one's economic and social capital is related to cultural capital: dispositions, mannerisms, and tastes; the consumption and accumulation of cultural goods; and education, in the form of institutional credentials and informal training (Bourdieu 1986). These attributes, knowledge, and ways of thinking can be used to accumulate additional social and economic advantages and "yield profits of distinction for its owner" (Bourdieu 1986:245). This book examines how white and Latina women's knowledge and dispositions relate to their entrepreneurial success. We know that in the business, legal, and scientific arenas, women's careers are often hindered by male-oriented workplaces (Martin 1994; Scott 1996; Swan 1994; Wright 1996). Compared to women of color, white women have made the greatest gains in achieving positions with higher earnings, authority, and advancement potential. Women and men of color face additional constraints of racial discrimination and informal barriers to advancement (Collins 1989; Higginbotham 1994; Martin 1994). A closer exploration is needed of the workings of cultural capital for the experiences of women entrepreneurs. What cultural capital do white and Latina women feel is necessary for success in business ownership?

CONCLUSION

Our economy represents a social space in which women entrepreneurs increasingly enter and actively pursue the profits and rewards it offers. This social space, however, is not gender, race, or class neutral. Women's economic activities, the paid and unpaid work they do, take place within the context of gendered ideologies. Women in the United States overwhelmingly hold lower-paid jobs in comparison to men, continue to do the bulk of unpaid household work, and are increasingly becoming impoverished, single heads of households. Through this book, I illustrate that, on the one hand, women's entrepreneurship is structured by society's differential distribution of capital. On the other hand, women also strive to maximize their capital for economic gain.

Women are not all "equally disadvantaged" within the labor market. Class societies continue to be marked by differences of economic access that are "secured and legitimated by reference to the natural features of the workers (age, race, sex, gender) in order to keep down the cost of labor power (the only source of value) and thus increase the level of profit" (Ebert 1996:91). Depending on their location in the social landscape, their social class and ethnic and racial background, some working women may have an advantage over other women and men in their access to resources needed to capture labor market positions. Such resources may also assist in the formation of businesses.

This book explores business ownership among white and Latina entrepreneurs who operate businesses in the formal U.S. economy. In the following chapter, I discuss nationwide trends of women's entrepreneurship, in addition to the study setting, methods of data collection, and participants. Chapter 3 examines the various pathways that women take to becoming business owners. Chapter 4 employs Pierre Bourdieu's forms of capital to assess women's use of capital in their entrepreneurship and questions how such capital might be gendered. In Chapter 4, I investigate how white and Latina women obtain the start-up money for their businesses and who they turn to for business advice and assistance. I analyze how familialism and co-ethnic networks might relate to women's successful business ventures. Lastly, I incorporate Bourdieu's concept of cultural capital in order to analyze cultural resources that the women feel are necessary to succeed in business. Chapter 5 is devoted entirely to Latina women's entrepreneurship experiences.

CHAPTER 2

Women's Entrepreneurship in the U.S.

NATIONWIDE TRENDS

We have seen notable increases of women's entrepreneurship in the United States, particularly in the last few decades. As mentioned in Chapter 1, women now comprise a larger percentage of the self-employed and own considerably more firms in the United States. The 1972 Survey of Women-Owned Businesses was the first effort made by the U.S. Bureau of the Census to detail basic economic data on businesses owned by all women and minority firms owned by women in the United States. The Bureau of the Census considers a business to be woman-owned if the sole owner or half or more of the partners are women; or in a corporation, if 50 percent or more of the stock is owned by women. The 1972 survey found a total of 402,025 women-owned firms, representing 4.6 percent of all U.S. firms, and pulling in 0.3 percent of all receipts (U.S. Bureau of the Census 1976). In 1972, 33,810 minority-owned firms also were women-owned (U.S. Bureau of the Census 1976). At this time, women-owned firms were highly concentrated in selected services and retail trade. Personal services, miscellaneous retail, real estate, and eating and drinking places represented some of the largest major industry groups in receipts of women-owned firms.

By 1982, women had made impressive gains in their share of U.S. businesses. In 1982, there were 2.9 million women-owned firms in the United States, representing 23.9 percent of all business firms, and accounting for 10.2 percent of all business receipts (U.S. Bureau of the Census 1986). Similar to the 1970s, the majority of women-owned firms in 1982 were concentrated in selected services and retail trade. Personal services, real estate, and health services were among the largest major industry groups in receipts of women-owned firms.

In 1992, the number of women-owned firms jumped to 5.9 million, 34.1 percent of all U.S. firms, and representing 19.3 percent of all U.S. firm receipts (U.S. Bureau of the Census 1996a). Estimates including women-owned C corporations place the total number of women-owned firms at over 6.4 million in 1992. Nationwide, women's entrepreneurship continues to be high in services and retail trade compared to all U.S. firms. Table 2.1 indicates that just over half of all women-owned businesses in the U.S. operate as service businesses, most in personal, business, or social services, and about one fifth are classified as retail trade businesses, primarily in apparel and food stores, eating and drinking places, and miscellaneous retail stores (U.S. Bureau of the Census 1996a).

While women-owned firms cluster in services and retail trade, a second tier of gender segregation exists because women-owned businesses tend to be concentrated in the most "female" type fields, such as public relations, health, and beauty (Loscocco and Robinson 1991). Many of these operate in low-growth industries or highly competitive markets (Loscocco and Robinson 1991). Goffee and Scase (1985) find that women who are committed to conventional gender roles frequently start businesses, like beauty, catering, or cleaning agencies, using skills acquired through performing traditional women's roles. However, impressive gains have been made in the number of women-owned firms in the less traditional women business sectors. Between 1987 and 1992, the number of women-owned construction firms nearly doubled (U.S. Bureau of the Census 1996a).

Following the nationwide trend, the majority of women-owned firms have always operated as sole proprietorships. The proportion of women-owned sole proprietorships has decreased from 98 percent in 1972 to 86 percent in 1992 (U.S. Bureau of the Census 1996a, 1976). While only 14 percent of all women-owned firms nationwide have paid employees, the Small Business Administration (1995) estimates that small businesses owned by women in the United States provide more jobs than do all the Fortune 500 corporations put together.

Gross receipts of women-owned businesses remain significantly lower than those of men-owned firms. Using a national sample of 1980 sole proprietorship income tax returns, Loscocco and Robinson (1991) found that women's average business receipts lagged behind men's in every industrial category. Census data from 1992 indicates that 34 percent of all U.S. firms are women-owned, however, they generate only 19 percent of all receipts in the United States. Thirty-nine percent of women-owned firms have gross receipts of less than $5,000 annually (U.S. Bureau of the Census 1996a). The top industry receipt leaders for women-owned firms include wholesale trade, automotive dealers and gasoline service stations, miscellaneous retail, and business services (U.S. Bureau of the Census 1996a).

Table 2.1 Comparison of Women-Owned Firms and All U.S. Firms, 1992, by Major Industry Group

Major Industry Group	Women-owned Firms (N= 5 888 883)	All U.S. Firms (N=17 253 143)
Percent Distribution		
Agriculture, Forestry, Fishing	1. 5	3
Mining	0. 5	1
Construction	3	11
Special Trade Contract	72	76
Manufacturing	3	3
Transportation, Public Utilities	2	4
Wholesale Trade	3	3
Retail Trade	19	14
Finance, Insurance Real Estate	10	11
Services	54	45
Personal	21	16
Business	25	24
Social	14	8
Industries not classified	5	5

Source: U.S. Bureau of the Census 1996a. Table includes individual proprietorships, partnerships, and subchapter S corporations. Excludes "C" corporations. Percentages represent distributions within the next broader industrial category. For example, 54 percent of all women-owned businesses in 1992 were in services, and 10 percent of those in services are in health-related services. Percentages in industrial subcategories do not sum up to 100 because only selected categories are included.

Table 2.2 Women-Owned Businesses and all U.S. Firms, 1992, by Legal Form of Organization, Employees, and Receipts

Category	Women-owned Firms (N= 5 888 883)	All U.S. Firms (N=17 253 143)
Percent Distribution		
Legal Form of Organization		
Subchapter S Corps	9. 6	9. 1
Partnerships	4. 1	6. 3
Sole Proprietorships	86. 2	84. 6
Employment Size		
No Paid Employees	86. 1	81. 8
Paid Employees	13. 9	18. 2
Total, Sales and Receipts		
Less than $5,000	39. 2	30. 3
$5,000 to $9,999	16. 4	14. 2
$10,000 to $24,999	17. 8	17. 8
$25,000 to $49,999	9. 2	11. 3
$50,000 to $99,999	6. 5	9. 4
$100,000 to $249,000	5. 7	8. 7
$250,000 to $499,999	2. 5	4. 0
$500,000 to $999,999	1. 4	2. 2
$1,000,000 or more	1. 3	2. 3

Source: U.S. Bureau of the Census, 1996a. Table with census data includes individual proprietorships, partnerships, and subchapter S corporations. Excludes "C" corporations.

We must be cautious when examining gross business receipts, considering that the previously mentioned studies do not separate businesses that are part-time or sideline endeavors from those that are full-time. A striking proportion of self-employed women compared to men work part-time (45 percent and 18 percent, respectively) (Bregger 1996). Considering that most women-owned firms are run by self-employed individual proprietors, it seems reasonable that many could be part-time endeavors, which would significantly affect their receipts.

THE STUDY SETTING

As more and more women participate as business owners in the U.S. labor market, I wanted to understand how gender shapes women's pathways to entrepreneurship and the capital to which they have access. The remainder of this chapter offers a detailed look at the research methods used in this study and constructs a profile of study participants and their businesses.

I conducted this study in San Diego, California, which provides an exemplary setting for the study of women entrepreneurs. San Diego is the second largest county in California with a population of more than 2.6 million. The County covers approximately 4,255 square miles—65 miles from north to south and 85 miles from east to west (Office of Public Affairs 1993). Sixty five percent of its residents are white, 20 percent Latino, 7 percent Asian, and 6 percent African American (Office of Public Affairs 1993).

About one fourth of San Diegans are employed in the services industry (*Sandag Info* 1997). Retail trade, government, and manufacturing are other important employment industries. Roughly 9 percent of San Diegans are employed in the military (*Sandag Info* 1997). There are several important San Diego regional employment clusters that include interrelated industries driving wealth creation primarily through export of goods and services. San Diego employment clusters experiencing the most growth from 1990 to 1996 include recreational goods manufacturing, biotechnology and pharmaceuticals, communications, software and computer services, entertainment and amusement, and environmental technology (*Sandag Info* 1998).

San Diego County has a large number of businesses owned by white and Latina women. In the County, there are over 67,000 women-owned firms, accounting for 8 percent of the total 800,000 women-owned firms in California (U.S. Bureau of the Census 1996a). California has the largest number of minority women-owned firms in the nation (U.S. Bureau of the Census 1996a). Minority women own over 97,000 businesses in California, of which most (44 percent) are owned by Asian women, followed by Latina, African American, and Native American women (38, 18, and .01 percent, respectively) (U.S. Bureau of the Census 1991). There are over 6,200 minority women-owned businesses in San Diego County, the greatest proportion of which are owned by Latinas (U.S. Bureau of the Census 1991).

Perhaps because of San Diego's relatively young economy, women have established firms in a diversity of industries, both traditional and nontraditional, throughout the County. Like women-owned businesses nationwide, those in San Diego tend to cluster heavily in services (58 percent), but they also have substantial representation in the fields of retail trade (16 percent) and finance, insurance, and real estate (12 percent) (U.S. Bureau of the Census 1996a). The five largest San Diego area women-owned businesses include a travel agency, a hotel, a temporary staffing agency, a shopping and dining complex, and an aerobic dance fitness franchisor (*San Diego Business Journal* 1997).

METHODS

When studying women entrepreneurs, I was faced with the question of how to reach these women business owners and collect information about their lives and enterprises. I began by meeting with some women entrepreneurs face-to-face. I used a number of different avenues for contacting the women whom I initially interviewed. Through Small Business Administration functions, San Diego County Minority Women Enterprise and Chamber of Commerce lists, and referrals, I found about a dozen women entrepreneurs who agreed to speak with me.

I also selected participants from the county-wide directory of fictitious business names for San Diego County, 1991–1997, which includes all sole proprietorships and partnerships operating legally in San Diego County. While this directory offers the most complete listing of businesses operating formally in San Diego County, it has some notable drawbacks. I used a computerized directory of the fictitious business list to construct a sample of white and Latina women business owners. Due to computer program limitations, this was a problematic task and by no means resulted in strict probability sampling. The computerized listing does not allow the entire fictitious business list to be viewed at once, nor does it offer any way to count or order the thousands of locally owned businesses. Even if one enters a letter on the owner inquiry name line, only the first 200 names (20 screens of 10 names) under that letter are displayed. Despite these difficulties, I used random numbers to determine where I would enter the list and to guide my selection of female names once I pulled up the listing screens. In order to arrive at a useable sample of Latina business owners, I oversampled them.

The fictitious business list also presents limitations because it does not document businesses that are incorporated. Still, 12 women (13 percent of my sample) with incorporated businesses participated in my study. Because they had renewed their fictitious business name recently enough, some continued to appear on the fictitious business list even though their businesses were incorporated. Incorporation offers business owners several advantages, including limited liability, freely transferrable shareholder interests, a stable appearance, and perpetual existence. For these reasons, incorporated businesses tend to be larger in terms of revenue and employees than sole proprietorships. Still, many entrepreneurs choose to establish sole proprietorships rather than incorporate their businesses because of the low start-up costs, few government requirements, autonomy, and tax benefits (avoiding double taxation). Because the fictitious business list does not catalog incorporated businesses, my sample is likely biased toward smaller companies. However, since such a small percentage of women-owned firms are incorporated (10 percent are subchapter S corporations which offer the advantage of avoiding double taxation), I presume this represents a minimal bias in my sample overall.

Another drawback of the computerized, fictitious business directory is that it lists the owner's name, business name and address, but not the phone number. It was often difficult to track down business phone numbers—a process that involved looking in various phone and business directories or dialing information for assistance. Further, some businesses that I called no longer had phone numbers. A computerized voice stated, "We're sorry you have reached a number that has been disconnected or no longer in service." There were no other business listings for them, and I presume that these have gone out of business. Because owners only need to refile their fictitious business names every five years, the most current directory I used included filings from 1991 to 1997. Knowing that a substantial portion of businesses don't make it past the first year, it is likely that some of those businesses who filed for licenses in 1991–1992 are no longer in operation.

Despite such problems with the fictitious business list, this study makes an important contribution by attempting to sample a wider range of businesses and business owners than many other studies on women's entrepreneurship. Previous studies focusing on local business owners have sampled entrepreneurs affiliated with formal networking organizations (Aldrich et al 1995; Staber and Aldrich 1995) or have conducted intensive interviews with relatively small numbers of women (Dallalfar 1994; Goffee and Scase 1985).

I was able to track down phone numbers for 195 of the 250 women business owners I selected from the County fictitious business list. From the fictitious business list, I successfully contacted 183 of these women-owned businesses and achieved a participation rate of 43 percent from the list. My initial contact with the women was over the phone. Perhaps the participation rate might have been higher if I had contacted these women initially through a letter, then followed up with a phone call. When cold calling the women, it was often difficult to make it past the secretary and speak with the owner. If I did, it was likely that they would give me the interview. In fact, only 12 of the women with whom I spoke stated that they did not want to participate. Still, for many of the businesses I called, there were secretaries or answering machines that prevented me from speaking directly with the owner. All the women who called me back expressed interest in the study and were interviewed.

Table 2.3 indicates that a total of 79 women from the fictitious list agreed to be interviewed. The other ten women in my sample were found using several different avenues, including Small Business Administration functions, business directories, and referrals.

Table 2.3 Number of Businesses Contacted and Number of Study Participants by Ethnicity in My Study, 1997.

Ethnicity	Number of Businesses Contacted Using Fictitious List	Number of Study Participants From Fictitious List	Participants from Other Avenues	Total Study Participants
Latina	46	19	3	22
White	137	60	7	67
Total	183	79	10	89

Of the 89 women in my final sample, 22 were Latina and 67 were white. From the fictitious business list, 41 percent of the Latina entrepreneurs whom I contacted followed through with an interview. In comparison, I had a 44 percent participation rate among white women entrepreneurs whom I called from the directory list. I had a slightly harder time obtaining interest from Latina women. I think I was at more of a disadvantage with Latina women for several reasons. After I explained that I was interviewing women business owners for my doctoral research at the University of California, Irvine, at least three Latina women expressed confusion over what a dissertation was. I explained that it was academic research and that their names would not be used in any way, but I still felt an element of doubt and distrust. Perhaps if I had also been Latina or bilingual, I might have been able to bridge some of this trust gap. When studying immigrant Iranian women business owners, Dallalfar (1994) found that being an Iranian woman and speaking Persian assisted her in developing rapport and agreement for participation. The race, class, and gender of a researcher can often be a crucial factor in gaining an individual's trust, interest, and participation in a study.

I conducted face-to-face interviews with 18 women entrepreneurs in this study. I met with these women in their places of business and each interview lasted approximately one to one and a half hours. Talking with the women face-to-face allowed me to probe into their backgrounds and family dynamics in addition to the characteristics of their businesses. I asked the women about their life histories, including where they grew up, the occupations of their parents, the schools they attended, their childhood aspirations for the future, and their past educational and occupational experiences. I then asked questions regarding their pathways to entrepreneurship, and asked them to elaborate on the factors or people influencing their business ownership. We also discussed their sources of start-up capital and financial support, mentors, advice and assistance networks, and mannerisms and behaviors within business networks that make a good impression.

I gained valuable insight by going to these women's places of business because it gave me an opportunity to view the business setting and layout. For example, just speaking with Patty Rogers over the phone did not allow me to understand the extent to which her business and family life were integrated. I didn't realize she had a home-based business until she gave me directions to her home office. Without visiting Vicki Torres' place of business, I would not have known that, while she spends much of her time at her desk in an office, most of her employees are blue-collar men who work in a communal area in a warehouse-like setting. My face-to-face meetings with most of these women felt very comfortable. The majority of women I spoke with were older than me, and they would often slip in words of advice for me and other working women in general. All of the women allowed me to tape record our conversations and take notes.

After completing the first 18 face-to-face interviews, I then conducted 71 telephone interviews that were not tape recorded. The telephone interviews were more structured than the face-to-face interviews. I asked a combination of open- and closed-ended questions that inquired about their sociodemographic and business characteristics, their reasons for becoming a business owner, their sources of economic capital, their use of assistance networks, and gender- or race-related advantages or disadvantages of entrepreneurship. Most telephone interviews lasted between 25 and 30 minutes, but in a couple of cases the interviews lasted closer to 45 minutes.

All of the 89 women in my study currently owned and operated at least 50 percent of their businesses. It was important for me to interview women who not only had ownership on paper, but also were involved in the daily activities of running a business. In addition, I included only those women whose businesses represented their primary form of employment, rather than a sideline, temporary, or part-time endeavor. My decision to interview women who have chosen business ownership as a primary form of employment relates directly to the objectives of this study. When examining women's pathways to business ownership and how women's strategic use of capital impacts their businesses, it makes little sense to compare women with full-time businesses to those who maintain sideline businesses in which they spend a few hours per month. It is likely that women who have part-time or sideline businesses devote considerable time to other employment or family-related activities. Certainly their business needs, concerns for growth and revenue, and future goals are fundamentally different from women who are fully engaged in entrepreneurial activities. Therefore, I chose to limit the scope of this study to women entrepreneurs who live with the day-to-day pressure of maintaining a business.

THE STUDY PARTICIPANTS

Table 2.4 compares sociodemographic information for the Latina and white women in my study. Five Latina women were born outside the United States: four in Mexico and one in Japan due to her father's military service. All except for one, Eva Cruz, moved permanently to the United States when they were preschool age. In the case of Eva, she went to high school in the U.S., but didn't move here permanently until she was married at age 20. Four of the 67 white women were foreign born; three came from Western European countries and one was born in Africa of British parents. All were preschool age when they moved to the United States permanently, except for Maureen Davis who moved to the U.S. from Denmark when she was in her twenties.

Table 2.4 Sociodemographic Variables for Latina and White Women in My Study, 1997

Variable	Latina (N=22)	White (N=67)	Total Sample (N=89)
Percent Distribution			
Born in the United States	77. 3	94. 0	89. 9
Age			
25–34	18. 2	14. 9	15. 7
35–44	13. 6	40. 3	33. 7
45–54	54. 5	35. 8	40. 4
55–64	9. 1	7. 5	7. 9
65 and over	4. 5	1. 5	2. 2
Marital Status			
Never Married	22. 7	14. 9	16. 9
Married	68. 2	58. 2	60. 7
Divorced	9. 1	26. 9	22. 5
Of Married Women, Percent with Husband Integrated in Business	46. 7	23. 0	29. 6
Children (Currently)			
None	27. 3	47. 8	42. 7
Dependents (<18)	18. 2	22. 4	21. 3
Adults (>18)	54. 5	29. 9	36. 0
Education (Highest Level)			
High School Diploma	31. 8	16. 4	20. 2
Some College	22. 7	22. 4	22. 5
Bachelors Degree	40. 9	38. 8	39. 3
Graduate Degree	4. 5	22. 4	18. 0

Note: All women in my sample were full-time workers due to sample design.

The largest proportion of women in this study were ages 45 to 54. Only 16 percent were between ages 25 and 34. Proportionally, more of the Latina than white women were over age 45 (68 and 45 percent, respectively). Self-employment is increasingly common as one gets older. The largest amount of self-employment tends to occur in midcareer. Advanced age and education appear to be strong determinants of both women's and men's self-employment relative to wage-and-salaried work (Carr 1996). Younger people are less likely to be self-employed because they may lack the skills and financial resources necessary to start a business.

Most of the women (61 percent) in my study were married. A larger proportion of Latina women were married and a smaller proportion were divorced compared to the white women in my sample. Married Latina women were more likely to have their husbands integrated into their businesses than their married white counterparts (47 and 23 percent, respectively). Half the women did not have children at the time of opening their businesses, however, that percentage dropped (to 43 percent) when asked if they had children currently. Thirty six percent of the women currently have children over age 18; one fifth have dependent children. A higher proportion of Latina women compared to white women in this study have children.

All of the women in my study had graduated from high school and most had earned bachelors degrees. The educational attainment for Latina compared to white women was lower. Latinas were two times more likely than white women to have earned only a high school diploma. Equal percentages of white and Latina women took some college courses, but did not graduate with a college degree. While the proportion of Latina women who earned bachelors degrees is slightly higher, white women were five times more likely to have earned a graduate degree than Latinas.

My sample is slightly older than the national average for self-employed women. Table 2.5 shows that of the almost 4 million self-employed women in the United States surveyed in 1994, most were in mid-career (age 35 to 44). A higher percentage of self-employed women nationwide are married compared to my sample. It also should be noted that the data on self-employed women nationwide includes both full- and part-time workers, whereas my sample includes women who work full-time in their businesses. This might explain some of the difference in sociodemographic characteristics between my sample and the nationwide data.

**Table 2.5 Self-Employment in the United States, by Selected
Characteristics, 1994**

Characteristic	Self-Employed Women (N=3, 891, 000)
Percent Distribution	
Age, Years	
16–19	2. 0
20–24	3. 0
25–34	20. 0
35–44	29. 0
45–54	23. 8
55–64	14. 4
65 and Older	7. 8
Marital Status	
Never Married	7. 3
Married, Spouse Present	74. 7
Previously Married	18. 0
Full- or Part-Time	
Full-Time Workers	55. 2
Part-Time Workers	44. 8

Source: Bregger 1996.

THE BUSINESSES IN THE STUDY

Most of the women in my study run businesses in the broad services industry
(Table 2.6). Several noticeable differences emerge when comparing women-
owned businesses in my study and those nationwide. My sample has a higher
percentage of women in services. Three-fourths of the businesses in my sample
are service oriented. Most of the services business in my study are business or
personal services. Business services typically include public relations or
business management consulting, training and development services, personnel
firms, and computer services. Personal services businesses in this study include
domestic cleaning businesses, photographic services, beauty and massage
services, and wedding and party planning. There are similar percentages of
women in my study and nationwide who operate retail and wholesale trade and
construction firms. I have a slightly smaller percentage of women in my study
who are in manufacturing, and I did not interview anyone in agriculture, mining,
or transportation. These differences can be explained, in part, by San Diego's
large service and financial sectors. My impression was that owners of service-
related businesses seemed to be more willing to participate and give me time
over the phone than others. This might be due to the fact that many of these
women conduct business over the phone and were comfortable with the idea of a
phone interview. Some women in retail seemed a bit more reluctant. Several

women in retail who agreed to participate interrupted our telephone interviews to assist customers.

Table 2.6 Business Characteristics for Latina and White Women in My Study, 1997

Business Characteristic	Latina (N=22)	White (N=67)	Total Sample (N=89)
Percent Distribution			
Industrial Category			
Construction	4. 5	0. 0	1. 1
Manufacturing	4. 5	0. 0	1. 1
Wholesale Trade	0. 0	1. 5	1. 1
Retail Trade	31. 8	3. 0	10. 1
Finance, Insurance, Real Estate	4. 5	11. 9	10. 1
Services	54. 5	83. 6	76. 4
Personal	16. 7	25. 0	23. 5
Business	75. 0	64. 3	66. 2
Health		10. 7	8. 8
Age of Business			
Less than 5 Years	18. 2	59. 7	49. 4
Five to Ten Years	36. 4	17. 9	22. 5
More than Ten Years	45. 5	22. 4	28. 1
Number of Employees			
None	50. 0	68. 7	64. 0
Less than 10	45. 5	20. 9	27. 0
Ten or More	4. 5	10. 4	9. 0
Gross Receipts or Sales			
Less than $25,000	4. 5	12. 1	10. 2
$25,000–$99,999	54. 5	59. 1	58. 0
$100,000–$499,999	27. 3	18. 2	20. 5
$500,000 and Over	13. 6	10. 6	11. 4

Note: Percentages represent distributions within the next broader industrial category. For example, 76. 4 percent of women-owned businesses were in services, and 23. 5 percent of those in services are in personal services. Percentages in industrial subcategories do not sum up to 100 because only selected categories are included. I did not interview any women who had businesses in agriculture, transportation, or mining.

Most of the businesses owned by women in my study are sole proprietorships or legal partnerships; 13 percent are incorporated businesses. Almost half of my sample have been in business less than five years. Latina women tended to be in business longer than the white women. Almost half of Latinas have owned their businesses for more than 10 years, compared to about one-fifth of white women. Fifty percent of the Latina women in my sample have paid employees compared to about one-third of white women (Table 2.6). Keep in mind that the Latina women were older than their white counterparts in my study, which might explain variations in age of business and employees.

The financial information I obtained regarding women's businesses was confined to gross sales or receipts. Rather than asking them for an exact dollar amount, I had them place their gross business sales or receipts within a numerical range (e.g., less than $5,000, between $5,000 and $9,999, etc). In my 1997 study, the largest proportion of women-owned businesses generated $25,000 to $100,000 in annual gross receipts or sales (Table 2.6). In contrast, most nationwide women-owned businesses generated less than $10,000 annually in gross receipts in 1992 (U.S. Bureau of the Census 1996a). My study was conducted five years later than the most recent Census data available at the time, but it seems likely that a substantial amount of the difference in the figures can be explained by the fact that the Census does not differentiate between women's full-time and part-time business endeavors. Similarly, this might explain why a higher proportion of my sample has employees compared to the nationwide figures.

CONCLUSION

A broad overview of women's entrepreneurship finds that most women-owned firms in the United States cluster in the services and retail trade industries and operate as sole proprietorships without employees. Over 50 percent of such firms have gross receipts of less than $10,000 annually. Although we don't have national data separating women's part- and full-time business endeavors, we do know that a large proportion of self-employed women work part-time.

Attempts to dissect this larger picture are crucial in order to understand fully women's entrepreneurship. This book analyzes one part of the overall picture by focusing exclusively on a specific group of women entrepreneurs: those who are fully engaged with their businesses as full-time employment. In keeping with the national trend, most of the women in my study have sole proprietorships, without employees, in the services or retail trade industries. My sample differs significantly from the national data on women's business gross receipts and sales. The largest proportion of businesses owned by women in this study generate gross annual receipts of between $25,000 and $100,000. This difference is largely due to my focus on full-time businesses, a focus that adds considerably to our knowledge of entrepreneurship because, by separating out part-time firms, it offers information that can provide more meaningful comparisons between full-time women-owned and all U.S. firms. The chapters that follow explore why women entrepreneurs enter into business for themselves and examine the capital they use to sustain such endeavors.

CHAPTER 3

Women's Pathways to Entrepreneurship

WHAT FACTORS LEAD TO ENTREPRENEURSHIP?

There have been a number of approaches in the literature addressing why entrepreneurs launch their businesses. Many of these studies are based on conclusions drawn from studying men. Research on entrepreneurship has investigated social and psychological factors related to entrepreneurs' motives for starting a business. One important motive appears to be the desire for personal autonomy, independence, and job freedom (Bechhofer et al. 1974; Scheinberg and MacMillan 1988). Other commonly cited reasons for entrepreneurs to set up their own businesses are dissatisfaction with previous work experience or loss of employment (Chinoy 1955; Scase and Goffee 1982; Shapero 1975). While these studies suggest that individuals are often pushed into entrepreneurship by negative occurrences, other research indicates that pull factors, like potentially profitable business opportunities, attract individuals into entrepreneurial activities (Jenssen and Kolvereid 1992; Moore and Buttner 1997).

More recent research focusing on women entrepreneurs suggests other reasons for becoming an entrepreneur. Theresa Devine (1994) argues that a woman's decision to become self-employed appears "intricately linked with several other decisions for a woman—as an individual, as a household member, at a point in time, and over the course of her life" (p. 33). Devine's analysis of 1990 Current Population Survey data reveals that the average self-employed woman is older, more likely to be married, and to be in a managerial or administrative occupation compared to the average wage-and-salary woman. Brush (1992) suggests that a woman's decision to start a business and her business relationships are more integrated into her life and influenced by strong linkages between work and family. Carr (1996) also finds that marital status and family characteristics, such as having young children, are strong predictors of women's self-employment. These studies are significant because they make a contribution to our understanding of women entrepreneurs, a little researched topic until recently. However, a shortcoming of these studies is that they do not differentiate between women of different racial and ethnic backgrounds. My study compares and contrasts the pathways to entrepreneurship for white and Latina women.

Most of the women in my study (92 percent) were employed full-time in the labor market immediately before establishing their businesses. As Table 3.1 indicates, most of these women were in executive or managerial, sales, or other service occupations. The highest percentage of white women had held executive or managerial positions, followed by sales and other service jobs. In contrast, the highest percentage of Latina women came from sales jobs, followed by executive and managerial jobs, and other service positions. None of the Latinas had previously been employed in professional specialties; however, almost one fifth of the white women had most recently held a professional position.

Table 3.1 Occupations of Women Prior to Establishing Their Own Businesses by Ethnicity in My Study, 1997

Occupation	Ethnicity	
	White (N=67)	Latina (N=22)
Percentage Distribution		
Executive, Managerial	23.9	22.7
Professional Specialty	17.9	0.0
Technical	4.5	0.0
Sales	20.9	27.3
Administrative Support	3.0	13.6
Private Household Service	2.9	0.0
Other Service	20.9	22.7
Not Employed	6.0	13.6

In attempting to uncover the various reasons why women enter business ownership, I asked each woman several open-ended questions: What prompted you to go into business for yourself? Why did you establish a business in this particular industry? What was going on with your family life when you decided to open a business? I find five primary reasons for women becoming entrepreneurs: responding to family-related concerns, leaving inflexible bureaucracies, being laid off, reacting to workplace discrimination, and capitalizing on opportunities to buy out existing ventures.

Table 3.2 Relationship between Primary Reason for Starting a Business and Ethnicity in My Study, 1997

Reason	Ethnicity		
	White (N=67)	Latina (N=22)	Total Sample (N=89)
Percentage Distribution			
Family-Related Concerns	34. 3	45. 4	37. 0
Phi coefficient 0. 10			
Homebased, Kids	16. 4	18. 2	16. 9
Partnership with Family	13. 4	22. 7	15. 7
Divorce	4. 5	4. 5	4. 5
Inflexible Bureaucracies	32. 8	4. 5	25. 8
Phi coefficient 0. 28*			
Layoff	17. 9	36. 4	22. 5
Phi coefficient 0. 19			
Workplace Discrimination	10. 4	0. 0	7. 9
Phi coefficient 0. 17			
Right Timing and Opportunity	4. 5	13. 6	6. 7
Phi coefficient 0. 16			

Note: * Fisher's exact test significant at 0. 01 level. Other tests not statistically significant.

BUSINESS OWNERSHIP AS A RESPONSE TO FAMILY CONCERNS

Over one third of the women in this book chose to enter business ownership due to family-related concerns. I divide these concerns into three main areas: starting home-based businesses to have flexibility for the needs of young children, establishing a partnership with a family member, and beginning a business for income after a divorce.

Needing Flexibility for Young Children Home-based businesses appear to offer a convenient and flexible way for mothers with young children to work for pay. About half of the women who cited family concerns (15 of the 33) as a pathway to business ownership had pre- or school-age children at the time of starting their businesses. All run businesses out of their homes. Self-employment is a strategy used by working women to combine home and work responsibilities. Carr (1996) found that women with preschool children were more likely than childless or the mothers of school-age children to be self-employed.

The phenomenon of women doing business at home in order to generate income while attending to domestic responsibilities is nothing new. Many early nineteenth-century families operated as small businesses and looked to women and children to contribute to the family economy: women took in boarders and lodgers to supplement family income, and children often took apprenticeship positions (Gerson 1985). In such cases economic life closely coincided with family life.

In the United States, the growth of industrialization and urbanization brought about changes in family relations and men's and women's gender roles. Most households were no longer productive units. To a large extent, economic production and family life became separated from each other. Barbara Rogers (1980) details how the function of households became that of consumer units, as more kinds of work were done outside the home and on a payroll. Even though in the early nineteenth century, factories employed men, women, and children, paid work was increasingly seen as the domain of men. Women were increasingly seen as housewives.

While these ideologies of men's and women's work still linger, today families in the United States are increasingly relying on the economic contribution of women who work for pay. In fact, over half of all women with children under age six work for wages (U.S. Bureau of the Census 1995). Affordable child care and maternity and paternity leave are often inadequate to serve the needs of many families in the United States (Polakow 1993). The result is that work, parenting, and family responsibilities often conflict.

Thirty-eight year old Samantha Hatch's experiences exemplify this conflict. Samantha grew up in the 1960s during a time in which "dads went to work and moms were housewives." Samantha recalls, "There were divisions of labor that put me in the domestic role. I ended up doing all the inside stuff and my brother was out with dad. That didn't really happen until late grade school and I remember that vividly as a child." Shortly after earning a bachelors degree in psychology and a masters in the early 1980s, Samantha married Steve. After having their first child, Samantha recalls the difficulties of having a full-time job in the labor force and a young child:

> It was one of the most stressful times because I was presented with the great challenge of how to mother and work full-time. And I did it for three years and it was extremely difficult. I found I couldn't keep up with the work load on both sides because I basically had taken on another full-time job without any extra help. And he [Steve] was off working on his masters and working full-time and while we thought we had this wonderful egalitarian marriage, once we had children we came to discover there was definitely a difference in, there were different expectations.

Still prevalent in American society is the ideology that domestic concerns and child care should largely be the priority of women. Women have consistently been primarily responsible for domestic production and reproduction, and men for supporting the household with income (Beechey 1978; Eisenstein 1979; Hartmann 1979). The ideology of reproduction defining women in terms of wife-mother supports this gender division of labor (Chodorow 1979; Hochschild 1989). Arlie Hochschild (1989) finds this especially true of the women in her study. She reveals how working women confront the difficulties of a second shift in the home because American culture still confers on them primary responsibility for child rearing and household chores. "All in all, if in this period in American history, the two-job family is suffering from a speed up of work and family life," Hochschild (1989) argues, "Working mothers are its primary victims" (p. 9). Hochschild finds that some working women resent their husbands for not doing an equal share of the housework. Other women in her study also appear to pay the emotional price of devaluing themselves or their daughters as females. Hochschild (1989) elaborates, "The more important cost to women is not that they work the extra month a year; it is that society devalues the work of the home and sees women as inferior because they do devalued work" (p. 261).

Regardless of their domestic status, women tend to be viewed by their employers, and often view themselves, as actual or potential wives and mothers whose primary obligation is to their families not employers (Beechey 1978; Hartmann 1979; Tiano 1994). For Samantha, believing that a woman should be a mother first and worker second posed difficult challenges. With little child care help from her spouse, Samantha explains that it was one of the most stressful times. When she became pregnant the second time, Samantha decided to find work that she could do and still be available to her children: "At this time, the type of work the company started doing, we would have contracts and bring in people as freelancers. So they brought me in a couple of times that first year." Rather than urging her husband to assist with housework and child care, Samantha cut back her hours at work. Hochschild (1989) also finds that many women in her study (52 percent) were not trying to change the gender division of labor in the household. Instead, they were either "supermoming," cutting back their hours at work, or cutting back at home.

Samantha took advantage of her employer's increased use of contingent workers by continuing as a part-time freelancer after giving notice. Increasing numbers of American workers, especially women, are hired on a contingent basis as part-time, temporary, or independent contracted workers (Christensen 1987). After working as a freelancer for about a year, Samantha established a home-based sole proprietorship in 1986.

Fourteen other women in this study also began home-based businesses in order to have more flexibility between paid work and domestic responsibilities. Thirty-one year old Kim McDonald established her business in 1996. The mother of two children under age 6, Kim underscores the flexibility offered by a home-based business:

> I have two small children. That's why I looked into a home-based business. It's flexible. I can volunteer at my daughter's school or take time to work out. If I was in a regular job in corporate America, I know that I'd be stressed out, sitting in traffic, with no quality time for myself or my children.

It is interesting that Kim equates a regular job with corporate America. The perception that Kim and many other Americans share is that work is something people leave the home to do. Many times work is associated with sitting in traffic jams, living with rigid time schedules, and spending 40–plus hours a week behind a desk in an office building.

Four Latina women established businesses in order to have more time for their children. Cynthia Valdes, 45 years old with three children under age 11, started a business partnership with her husband in 1983.

> A: Part of the impetus for starting the business was so that I could stay home and have flexibility with a family. In 1986 we had our first child. With having children, I wanted the flexibility of being home and raising the kids.

> Q: Was this also a consideration for your husband in having a home-based business?

> A: For him it was a question of overhead costs. Our goal was that as parents we wanted one of the two of us to have enough flexibility to be there for our children. I always wanted to be home for the children. And that's what's so good about being a business owner at home.

Cynthia confirms the important benefit of flexibility that comes from running a home-based business and having small children.

Husbands supported married women's decisions to own a business in order to provide income and spend more time with children. This is exemplified by the comments of 38-year-old Caroline Menard who started a secretarial services business in 1995. Caroline was employed as a secretary for 20 years before opening her own business. After their second child was born, Caroline's husband encouraged her to open up her own home-based business. "When I was still in the hospital recovering from having my daughter, my husband was out buying a computer for me to work at home," exclaims Caroline. She has found that having a home-based business allows her to attend to a number of activities.

A: I have a home-based business and the kids are at home with me. I take care of them.

Q: How old are your children?

A: One is two and a half. The other is five and a half. My son started kindergarten...I take care of them, work in my business, and my husband still wants me to cook dinner. And I cook dinner. It's good to have a business at home because you can deal with the house things.

Caroline's words suggest that her husband has greater decision-making power within the household. He urged her to work at home so she could devote time to the children, household chores, and business activities. As Caroline states, "I take care of them, work in my business, and my husband still wants me to cook dinner." And so, she cooks dinner. Caroline's story is indicative of many households in America in which married women work for pay and take responsibility for child care and housework (Hochschild 1989).

Caroline's and the other women's experiences illustrate how women use home-based businesses to be economically productive while also attending to reproductive activities in the domestic mode. This is an interesting reversal of the historical trend in which most households lost their role of productive unit and in which economic production and family life became increasingly separated. As in the early part of the country's history, more women today are turning to businesses in the home as a way to be active in economic production and domestic production and reproduction. This is not only the case with home-based businesses owned by women, but also women employed as homeworkers for industrial and manufacturing companies, as the case of Vermont women knitters (Boris 1987) and Hispanic immigrant garment homeworkers in the United States (Fernandez-Kelly and Garcia 1989).

The women in this book emphasize the positive aspects of having a home-based business, particularly the flexibility in balancing work and family. But, home-based work may also have disadvantages. Kathleen Christensen (1988) suggests that women who work at home often have trouble separating their roles as mothers and homemakers from their roles as wage earners. "The house itself constantly reminds them of what their homemaker selves could be doing" (Christensen 1988:162). Home-based work also can be isolating and sometimes is given less credibility than office work (Christensen 1988).

After opening their home-based real estate appraisal business in the 1980s, Doris and Roy Lamont felt that colleagues and clients viewed home-based businesses as less credible. "Years ago, we never said we worked at home," Doris explains,"There was a prejudice against that. There was a negative bias that you weren't as professional. You didn't have a "real" office." Doris believes that because more people have home-based businesses today, this negative bias has lessened in recent years.

Creating Partnerships with Family Whereas 15 women in my study started businesses to have more flexibility for their families, another 14 women, five Latina and nine white, responded to other family members who wanted to establish business partnerships with them.

Twelve of these women started partnerships with their husbands. Ann Ramos, a 41-year-old Latina with a degree in business, says, "After my children were grown, I saw the opportunity to start something up with my husband." Likewise, Sheila Murray started her career as an entrepreneur by taking over the family business with her husband: "I've almost always been an entrepreneur. I've run a stationary store and an electronic store. My husband and I bought the latest shop from my dad." After a lifetime as a business owner, 51-year-old Sheila also has started a consulting business and offers assistance to other women business owners.

Doris Lamont, who grew up in the Midwest, moved to California with her husband, Roy, in the late 1970s.

> I had been working for a couple of years as a paralegal in [Washington] D.C. I worked on one project that had a beginning and an end. When that ended, I was still with Roy and we decided that moving to California would be a good idea. We said, "Why not?" We were tired of what we were doing, we talked about getting into real estate.

Doris and Roy decided to move to San Diego because of the real estate boom at the time. After taking some courses at a local college and working with several local companies, Doris and Roy established a residential appraising business in 1986. The business is a home-based partnership. Their office consumes the second bedroom of their small, minimally furnished apartment.

Similarly, Patricia Stevens and her husband, Bill, established a business partnership together after moving from New York. Patricia grew up in Illinois and after high school, moved to New York and worked as a waitress for a number of years. After seeing an advertisement in the paper for makeup school, Patricia decided to enroll. Shortly after, Patricia married Bill, who works as a photographer. The couple decided to move to San Diego and started a photography business in 1994.

Claudia Sanchez and her husband Ricardo established their company together in 1991. Claudia is one of the most educated women in my sample. After graduating from a state university with a bachelors degree in engineering, Claudia worked for several years in a technical position at a large industrial company. It was there that Claudia met Ricardo. They were married in 1981, the same year that she won a graduate fellowship that enabled her to return to school and pursue a master's degree in engineering. Upon graduation, Claudia describes her first thoughts of becoming an entrepreneur:

A: We [Ricardo and I] were working in related fields and enough people said to us at cocktail parties and what not, "Claudia, what do you do? Ricardo what do you do?" And then they would say, "The two of you could go into business together. You do related things." And we would laugh about that and finally it started taking root and it seemed that we could have our own company, couldn't we? Between us the experience and the means to combine the service to major clients...I needed more knowledge about management, accounting and finance and marketing. I knew nothing about the business side. So I applied to business school.

Q: And your husband was supportive of that?

A: Yes. He wanted to start up a business in the future. He thought it was a good idea that one of us picked up those skills and he thought it would be better if it was me. So I was accepted and then he started a job in the area and I went to school. And as you go through the management program, they want you to take or choose a possible business that you are interested in and use it as your test case. Now, I used this company as my test case and created the research and business plan.

From her research, Claudia determined that the Southwest would be the best region in which to start their manufacturing business.

We found that in the Southwest, there was a higher proportion of start-up companies and newer technology involved in that. And we decided that that would be a better place to locate because then you don't have to replace a company's already established supplier to get into the market, you can start up along with those newer companies and become their supplier from the get go. And then that gets your foot in the door and then as your clients grow, your business grows.

Currently, Claudia and Ricardo have two employees. Their company grosses about $500,000 annually.

Cindy Kelley, 39 years old, decided to become a business owner after being approached by her uncle.

A: I had graduated from school with an art degree and I was looking for studio space. My uncle is also an artist and was looking for space, so we decided to go into business together. We had an art studio and a gallery. After three years into it, he dropped out of the business.

Q: Was this a difficult transition for you?

A: Not really. Uncle Mark wasn't able to handle a lot of the business part of what we did. He was almost deaf. But he was great at fixing things. He was so easy to get along with and we had few disagreements which was great. I'm apprehensive about bringing in someone else I don't know.

Responding to a Divorce Lastly, divorce also acted as a catalyst for four women to begin their own businesses. Sixty-one-year-old Maureen Davis started her business after her divorce at age 49. "I got divorced and I didn't just want to sit back and feel sorry for myself," says Maureen. "I kind of had my own business for 15 years teaching exercise classes, but there's no money in exercise. After the divorce I went to beauty school and started doing facials." Davis currently owns a health and beauty business that caters to prominent clients in a posh area of town. Nancy Parker, a 35-year-old florist with three school-age children, became a business owner shortly after her divorce:

I purchased the store after working in it for four years as an employee. The owner was selling and the opportunity presented itself so I went for it. I bought this business because I wanted to be able to educate my kids, to send them to college down the road if that's what they want to do. You don't make a lot of money in this industry unless you are an owner. So it was the motivation to send my kids to school.

Seventy-two-year-old Celia Robles also established her business in 1984, shortly after her divorce. Then age 59, she decided to establish a business in which she plays the violin at various local parties, openings, and exhibitions.

There are many musical groups who have been playing for years and years. They are already established and had no use for me. So I started the business...I have been playing music since age 11. It's my passion. My mother was in love with music, the piano.

Remarried in 1987, Gloria continues the business because, as Gloria puts it, "Social Security doesn't cut it."

In addition, Samantha Hatch, whom I have mentioned earlier, expanded her once part-time business into full-time after divorcing her husband four years ago. "When I divorced him, the business was no longer an option but a necessity," Samantha explains.

In sum, over one third of the women in this book decided to enter business ownership because of family-related concerns, such as having more flexibility for children, establishing a partnership with a family member, and beginning a business for income after a divorce. A higher proportion of Latina compared to white women entrepreneurs established businesses due to such concerns. In this study, Latina women were more likely than white women to establish home-based businesses to have flexibility for young children. A higher percentage of Latina compared to white women started businesses with a family member. The same proportion of white and Latina women chose to start businesses after a divorce.

LEAVING THE IRON CAGE

Prior to business ownership, many of the women had worked as waged or salaried employees in mid- to large-size bureaucracies. Some women's negative experiences within bureaucracies led them toward business ownership. When they were employed in large bureaucracies, some of the women in this study felt that their career potential was restricted and that their work schedules were too rigid.

Max Weber's (1946) classical statements on bureaucracy offer an important commentary on the constricting nature of bureaucratic organizations. Weber (1946) believed that contemporary society was increasingly grounded in the advancement of rationality and that the foremost example of rationality was the bureaucracy, which has a "purely technical superiority over any other form of organization" (p. 214). Weber identified several crucial elements of an ideal bureaucracy: an abstract legal code of conduct, specialized spheres of competence structured within a hierarchy of offices, and selection and promotion through qualification and proven ability.

Bureaucratization, according to Weber, offers the possibility of conducting business according to calculable rules, purely objective considerations, and without regard for persons. Weber (1946) argues that calculable rules are crucially important to the modern bureaucracy.

> The peculiarity of modern culture, and specifically of its technical and economic basis, demands this very "calculability" of results. When fully developed, bureaucracy also stands in a specific sense, under the principle of *sine ira ac studio*. Its specific nature, which is welcomed by capitalism, develops more perfectly the more the bureaucracy is "dehumanized," the more completely it succeeds in eliminating from official business love, hatred, and all purely personal, irrational, and emotional elements which escape calculation. This is the specific nature of bureaucracy and it is appraised as its special virtue (p. 215–16).

While Weber contends that bureaucracies are the most rational and efficient means for managing large groups of people, he still warns that bureaucracies could take on a life of their own and become iron cages within which workers feel little creativity or autonomy. The individual bureaucrat can feel like "a single cog in an ever-moving mechanism which prescribes to him an essentially fixed route of march" (Weber 1946:228).

Other scholars have emphasized the social relationships, the informal procedures within bureaucracies, and the barriers to advancement for social groups such as women and minorities that exist within bureaucracies (Jackall 1988; Kanter 1977). One such study is Rosabeth Moss Kanter's (1977) *Men and Women of the Corporation* in which she examines the ways bureaucratic structures form people's sense of themselves and of their possibilities.

> A large measure of the responsibility for the behaviors people engage in at work and their fate inside organizations lie in the structure of work systems themselves. . . . People are capable of more than their organizational positions ever give them the tools or time or opportunity to demonstrate (Kanter 1977:10).

Kanter demonstrates that responses to work are a function of basic structural issues such as the constraint imposed by roles and the effects of opportunity, power, and numbers. In explaining why women remain segregated in low-pay bureaucratic positions, like clerical and service personnel jobs, Kanter (1977) argues that "men at the top . . . are not necessarily part of a conspirational plot to keep women from power" (p. 263). Rather, they are responding to the organizational relations they have with women: "The dynamic of tokenism—the effects of limited numbers of women—make the women who do enter men's worlds operate at a disadvantage" (Kanter 1977: 263). Those women who do reach high-level corporate positions operate at a disadvantage due to high visibility and performance pressures, boundary heightening (men exaggerate their own commonality and the token's difference), and the use of stereotypes that result in the token's role encapsulation.

One fourth of the women in this book decided to become small capitalists after working in bureaucratic structures that they felt were inflexible and constraining. A significantly larger portion of white than Latina women turned to business ownership for this reason (33 and 5 percent, respectively).

These 23 women felt trapped within their previous positions, constrained by the structured work day and hours required of them, and held back by lack of promotion opportunities, not because of gender or ethnicity, but because of the rigid bureaucratic hierarchy. According to these women, gender and race/ethnic discrimination did not play a significant role in why they were held back from advancement. Rather, they talked about other white women and women of color, in addition to men, who were in higher positions and not planning to leave the organization. Due to the hierarchical structure, there were only so many higher positions. These women were tired of waiting for their opportunity.

The following comments were typical concerning bureaucratic workplaces:

> I wasn't happy in the corporate world. It's a world created by someone else. It's like here's your hole, now go sit in it. There isn't any personality.

> I always wanted to own my own company. I started the business because I wanted freedom and flexibility. I wasn't comfortable in a political environment like the newspaper and I wasn't able to move up in my last job.

> I wanted a job with more freedom and flexibility, a job so that when I do have a family, I don't have a boss telling me when I have to come and go.

> There's less friction running your own business. I do what I love, without the politics I loathe.

The experiences of 34-year-old Laura O'Neil typify those of others who perceived blocked upward mobility within rigid bureaucracies. Laura came from an entrepreneurial family.

> My parents, neither of them went to college. My dad was more of, well, he was in sales all of his life and now is a small business owner himself, and had been. So I think that might have had some influence.

After graduating from high school, Laura went to junior college and did freelance writing to "kind of keep afloat." Her internship at a local newspaper soon turned into a permanent staff research position in 1987. After five years, Laura transferred into the sales department and became a top producer within a couple of years.

> But there was no motivation for me to continue with them. And as far as a sales management position, which would have been my next step, I was senior account manager, that position seemed to be locked up for a while by a gal that the publisher really admired and she wasn't moving anywhere. So there wasn't advancement, so I actually kind of crashed physically and mentally.

Laura wanted more challenging work opportunities, but felt constrained within the confines of a bureaucratic workplace. Rather than attempt to find a similar position at another publisher, Laura established her own business in 1995.

What was transpiring, you know, is that I had mastered in my mind this whole sales process, so what I wanted was to take my editorial experience and my writing skills, my sales skills and then project management skills that I had gained. I wanted to take all that and kind of create my own publication.

Laura's business offers public relations and writing services. Recently divorced and without children, she often finds herself consumed by her work, spending "after working hours" on various client projects. Laura values the freedom that comes with being a sole proprietor, but this freedom can be lonely and bittersweet: "Cause now it's me living alone. It's me alone [in my business]. And it's me alone socially now without a partner. So all aspects of my life, now are just me and not shared."

Stephanie Ray established her business to escape the rat race of previous bureaucratic workplaces. Stephanie, now in her early 30s and single, has been in computer consulting since earning a bachelors degree in business. She opened her business in 1994.

I had worked for large companies for about 10 years and I just got really burned out on the long hours. I wanted more flexibility, and more time. My parents have always been self-employed, self-made people. My mom is a real estate broker and my dad is a developer. They gave me motivation. When I first graduated from college, I thought I wanted the corporate America job, but it didn't work out that way. Now I'm into this entrepreneurial venture. I didn't have concerns about success, that I would be successful, because I saw my parents go through a lot. It wasn't an unknown, starting a business.

Stephanie has followed in the footsteps of her parents who also are small business owners. She presently owns a computer information systems consulting business and, due to a substantial County contract, her company grosses between $200,000 and $500,000 annually. Within her first six months of business, Stephanie had hired 10 employees. The business growth means 50 to 60 hour work weeks for Stephanie. Still, she emphasizes other freedoms that business ownership brings, such as turning down work when clients are difficult.

Only one Latina in my sample, 54-year-old Eva Cruz, established her business primarily in response to the rigid schedule and fast pace of the workplace. Eva grew up in Tijuana, Mexico, and moved to San Diego with her husband in the 1960s. They currently live in a posh, upper middle class neighborhood with $500,000 homes. Married for 33 years with three grown children, Eva held a full-time, paid job through her marriage, except for a couple of years when her children were pre-school age. After working for a decade as a secretary, she decided to earn her bachelors degree in business.

I was working as a secretary and I was bored. I saw the type of people my boss hired for administrative jobs and I was more qualified than they were. But my boss said, "Yes, but you don't have a college degree and they do. To me a college degree means that you have persevered for four years. You have set a goal and met it."

Eva finished her degree. She was then promoted to a management position where she had previously been a secretary. Eva remained there for almost 10 years, and then was wooed away to a large, industrial firm by the promise of a higher salary and better position. But Eva soon tired of the long hours and demanding workload. "I had nightmares about it," explains Eva, "And I was wanting to just not work for anyone else. I was tired of the dynamic. I wanted to see what I could do on my own. I couldn't go back to management. I couldn't go back to being a secretary."

In 1991, at age 48, Eva opened a party planning business. "I have always planned parties. That was my hobby. And I cooked for the homeless and other charities." She has five employees: two part-time office assistants and three contract employees who she uses when planning and catering parties. Although her hours are varied and flexible, Eva still spends at least 40 hours per week on her business.

It is significant to mention that Eva's husband has been a small business owner since the 1960s, with a booming wholesale business that crosses into Central and South America. Having witnessed the entrepreneurial ventures of other close family members, Eva, Laura, and Stephanie viewed business ownership as a viable alternative to wage employment. Likewise, nine other women who turned to business ownership due to inflexible bureaucracies had entrepreneurial family members. Given the inflexibility of most workplace bureaucracies, these women chose to own businesses as opposed to working in someone else's. Despite the reality of long hours and catering to clients' schedules, this decision allows these women to feel a greater sense of control over their work lives.

These findings are consistent with Moore's and Buttner's study (1997) in which they interviewed over 100 women entrepreneurs who had previous corporate work experiences. Using survey and interview data from metropolitan areas nationwide, Moore and Buttner (1997) find that these women primarily established businesses because they were searching for the autonomy, freedom, and self-determination that was lacking in large organizational work settings. Important attractive qualities of operating one's own business included: respect and recognition for accomplishments, the opportunity to be in charge, and regaining feelings of excitement about work (Moore and Buttner 1997).

In sum, one fourth of the women entrepreneurs in this book became business owners after working in large bureaucracies they felt were inflexible and constraining. A significantly larger proportion of white compared to Latina women turned to business ownership for this reason (33 and 5 percent, respectively). Bivariate analysis suggests that there is some relationship between ethnicity and leaving a bureaucracy to become an entrepreneur (phi coefficient is 0.28 and Fisher's exact test is significant at the 0.01 level).

BEING LAID OFF

Over one fifth of the women turned to business ownership after being laid off from a previous wage or salary position. Most of the laid-off women lost their jobs in the 1980s and had been in business at least five years. More specifically, 45 percent of these women (a total of nine) had been business owners between five and 10 years, and 30 percent (a total of six women) had been business owners for more than 10 years.

Much attention has focused on the displacement of blue-collar industrial workers due to contemporary structural trends in the labor market: capital flight, deindustrialization, and the growth of the service sector of the economy (Eitzen and Baca Zinn 1989). One of the best known related studies is Barry Bluestone's and Bennett Harrison's (1982) *The Deindustrialization of America*. Bluestone and Harrison (1982) detail American corporate strategies since the 1970s to shift capital from one activity, one region, and one nation to another. They critique this process as "a tactic that management wished to have at its disposal in order to "discipline" labor and to assure itself of a favorable business climate wherever it set up operations" (Bluestone and Harrison 1982:16). A favorable business climate means lower wages, rates of unionization, worker safety standards, environmental regulations, and taxes. Bluestone and Harrison (1982) argue, "Only in the last two decades has systematic deinvestment become, from management's perspective, a necessary strategy, and from a technological perspective, a feasible one" (p. 16).

But blue-collar, industrial workers are not the only ones who lost their jobs in the past few decades. "We are used to the fact that our manufacturing industries are on the skids," notes social anthropologist Katherine Newman (1993), but "in the 1980s a new habit began to spread through corporate America, a tradition of declining loyalty of firm to worker and a consequent wariness among younger employees of depending upon any job for permanent security" (p. 14). Newman's (1988, 1993) research on downward mobility in the United States illustrates that more educated or credentialed workers have been affected by shakeouts and shutdowns in corporate America. Of the 5 million displaced workers in the United States between 1981 and 1986, 15 percent were managers or professionals and 22 percent held technical, sales, and administrative support positions.

Of the 20 women who spoke of being laid off as a route to entrepreneurship, 45 percent (nine women) were managers or professionals and 35 percent (seven women) were in service-related occupations. The remaining 20 percent (four women) had been in technical, sales, or administrative positions. Unlike women laid off from smaller companies or from low-paying positions, women from larger corporate environments or management positions (five of the 20) were compensated with severance packages. It is ironic that, for one-fourth of these laid-off women, the compensation they received from being laid off actually enabled them to start new careers in the form of business ownership. Laid-off workers find severance pay important for a number of reasons. It can "buy time for people who have to make major readjustments in their lives and relieves the pressure of immediate financial catastrophe. At the same time, it is a potent symbol of esteem" (Newman, 1988:50) This study finds another practical value of severance pay: start-up capital for new businesses.

Susan Freeman, a 44-year-old wedding coordinator, discussed her decision to start a business after being laid off in 1990 from a mid-size, local company:

> I had a weird predicament. Eighty percent of the work staff was given early retirement or a nice severance to leave. I was among the group they offered it to. None of us had to take it. It took me three months to decide. I had been there 14 years. It was a decent paying job. It was a tough decision, but if I didn't take it, I found that I would have wound up in a secretarial position working for a man I despised. I wasn't a secretary. I hate that work. My husband was basically saying, "You have to decide for yourself." What I'm doing now is where I should be.

Susan was able to use the money from being laid off in order to establish a business of her own.

Forty-nine-year-old Rachel Maxwell describes her first attempt at business ownership in the mid 1980s.

> I'm not a natural business woman, that's not me. In France I taught English as a second language and met my yoga teacher and got training. When I came back to the U.S., that's what I wanted to do. Yoga satisfies me. I got my certificate to be a yoga teacher and had a big party and invited people to come to the opening of my center. I go over the next day when I'm supposed to give the class and nobody showed up. Because I had no idea of the basics, of recruiting and finding students, no idea of target market. I had nothing. I mean somewhere between kindergarten and fourth grade.

Rachel decided to return to her profession of teaching, and after being laid off two years ago, she tried business ownership again.

> So I went back to teaching. So then, that was no longer any fun. I mean I taught yoga on the side, but not to make money. I'm responsible to yoga, and sort of, if you don't live out what you need to do, you get bored. I was starting to make less money. I wasn't happy teaching so therefore they didn't want me. You know, I didn't want to be there either. And I ended up when they had a downsizing, I lost my job, which of course, many people will say, "It was the best thing that ever happened." I mean, you know, if you are able to roll it over and create lemonade out of that.

Having been dissatisfied in her teaching career, it was not until after being laid off that Rachel tried once again to establish her own business as a yoga instructor.

Likewise, losing her job was the push that Renee Jackson, a 51-year-old psychotherapist, needed to establish her own business.

> I lost my job in 1990. I say I was given the golden boot of God. I use the arts in psychotherapy. I was at the point where I thought independence would be better anyway. People had been telling me for years to do it on my own.

Having worked for a carpet company that went out of business, 57-year-old Sue Desmond felt that she had enough experience to open up her own store.

> I found a job doing advertising sales. While I was there I ran into a carpet company. The guy running the business asked me if I liked what I was doing and asked me if I thought I could handle his business while he went away. I said, "Yes." I worked there for several years and then he closed the store. During my time there, I learned about flooring, painting, and installing. After he closed the store I said to my husband, "I think I'm going to open a carpet store." My husband said, "I'll give you a week." I had like ten cents to my name, but I started the business from my home, then moved into a shop.

Sue has been in business since the late 1970s. Many of the women discussed being laid off in a somewhat positive light: "People had been telling me for years to do it on my own" or "It was the best thing that ever happened." These women equate being laid off as becoming free to act upon their entrepreneurial aspirations. But for some women, losing their jobs posed significant financial burdens. As a result of these burdens, and perceptions that the labor market held few opportunities for them, some women turned to business ownership as a last resort for income.

Seventy-year-old Betty Simon is one of the oldest women in this study. Betty has a career history in graphic design, and in 1992, she was laid off from a large technical firm.

> I worked for a company that had been bought out. I was a matriarch of the firm. They effectively fired me, gave me the golden handshake. It was awful...I do not play bridge, own a TV, do not drink. I knew that I would have to occupy myself in some way. I opened my own business. I wasn't planning to leave [the previous company]. I knew that emotional and mental rigormortis would set in if I didn't do something. The main thrust is economic though. Since I spent my life raising three children alone, I knew I couldn't live off Social Security. I had to augment in some way, and this is the way.

For Betty, economic factors were a significant part of establishing her business. When Betty was given the golden handshake, she was in her mid 60s and saw few other job prospects in the labor market for a woman her age. Knowing that Social Security alone would not provide sufficient income, she established her graphic design business which she runs from her home. Her severance pay covered a substantial portion of the start-up costs: a computer, a copy and fax machine, drawing tables, bookcases, and file drawers.

A higher proportion of Latina women compared to white women started businesses after being laid off (36 and 18 percent, respectively). None of these Latina women received substantial severance packages. Four of these eight Latina women were laid off from service-related positions; two were in sales and two in management jobs. The experience of Gloria Morales, age 42, exemplifies some of the conditions surrounding Latina business ownership after losing a job. Gloria had worked as an employee at an employment agency before opening her own firm in 1994.

> I started out basically as the receptionist and office coordinator and pretty much doing everything that needed to be done, and it quickly evolved into staff meetings, and eventually I was made manager of the company. And so, I started in 1987 and he actually closed his doors and moved out of state in 1993.

Left without a job, Gloria sized up her employment options and decided that if she were going to stay in the industry, she wanted to start her own business and have control over policy and procedure. The opportunity arose, indirectly, out of her former employer's company.

A gentleman in the office next to my old office happened to be one of the owners of the complex and they initially were leasing agents and had their own mortgage company. When my ex-boss left, he left his old office site. . . . They wanted someone to help find people for their company, loan processors and people in the mortgage industry, so they asked me if I would do some placement work for them. That is how I got my start, and it just turned out that I used the office space and initially was interviewing people in restaurants.

Elaine Rodriguez is another Latina in this study who established a business after being laid off. Her experiences are similar to most other Latinas in the book who turned to business ownership due to lack of other options in the labor market. Elaine had worked in a firm in which she taught computer skills to employees.

In 1991 I was laid off by a large firm and I hesitated. I wasn't prepared to start a business for myself. I didn't have a lot of money, no cash flow. I was looking for a full-time job in the same type of work, but in 1991 the recession was bad. I was on unemployment benefits and I found myself saying, "I better get myself to work."

Elaine realized that finding a position working for someone else wasn't the most viable option. Like 70-year-old Betty Simon, Elaine turned to business ownership as an economic necessity, having perceived that adequate opportunities did not exist for her in the labor market. Whereas Betty associates age prejudice with her lack of job prospects, Elaine perceives that racial and ethnic discrimination have in some ways limited her job prospects and her opportunities as a business owner.

When I came here from Texas I wondered, "Where are they?" In San Antonio, the mayor was Hispanic, business people were Hispanic. Here, they're in fast food chains. When you lose your job, it really hits your confidence level. I thought, "I'm Hispanic and there's no way I'm going to get a contract.'

In San Diego County, Elaine argues that a kind of silent discrimination exists for Latinos, who cluster in low pay occupations. Many other Latinas spoke of racial and ethnic discrimination in San Diego's business community (detailed in Chapter 5). Latina women who establish independent business ventures after being laid off appear to start businesses as a way to work around obstacles that result from lack of opportunity within the labor market. This pattern also has been found among immigrant men who establish small businesses as a steppingstone to success (Light and Bonacich 1988; Portes and Bach 1985).

In sum, over one fifth of my sample turned to business ownership after being laid off from a previous wage or salary position. Most of the laid-off women lost their jobs in the 1980s and had been in business at least five years. A higher proportion of Latina compared to white women in this study started businesses after being laid off. None of these Latina women, however, received severance packages.

ESCAPING GENDER DISCRIMINATION

Seven women in this book established businesses to escape from gender discrimination in the workplace. All of these women were white, and five had previously held managerial or professional jobs.

Typically, women are concentrated in the lower tiers of managerial and professional occupations. Women managers, for example, tend to cluster in low level managerial jobs in small establishments in the service sector (Dunn 1997). However, the five women in my study from management or professional positions who emphasized discrimination as a pathway to entrepreneurship came from higher-status jobs with relatively high levels of reward.

In her 1977 study on organizational structure, Kanter found that women managers who reach higher-level positions experience special pressures due to their proportional rarity as token workers. First, women managers' higher visibility creates performance pressures for them. Second, male managers, those in the dominant group, are likely to exaggerate their own commonality and women's difference through displays of aggression or sexual teasing. Last, characteristics of women managers are often distorted to fit into preexisting generalizations. This leads women managers to be encapsulated into one of several stereotypical roles: the nurturing mother, the seductress, the peppy pet, or the tough, iron maiden (Kanter 1977).

Women are still grossly underrepresented in high level managerial positions, such as senior managers, vice presidents, or corporate officers, and they continue to experience pressures in such male-dominated environments (Rosener 1995). Few Latina women in this study were in male-dominated workplaces, and none previously had held high level management or professional positions. Consequently, they might not have experienced the unique pressures, such as boundary heightening and visibility, that the women in these positions associated with gender discrimination. This fact could explain why Latinas didn't emphasize gender discrimination as a reason for establishing their own businesses.

All five of the women previously in management and professional positions spoke of feeling like outsiders and separate from networks of male managers.

Typical statements included, ""They" did things for one another exclusively" and "I had run into glass ceilings throughout my career."

The experience of 55-year-old Keri Slater illustrates the ways that gendered beliefs in the workplace block women managers' advancement and lead them to entrepreneurship. Keri had worked for years in engineering-related occupations. Having earned her doctorate in the 1970s, she knows what it's like to be one of the few women working among men. In 1987, Keri was denied further management opportunities in a large scientific company.

> I thought, "I can beat my head against the wall and he'll [my boss] never give me the recognition I want and the opportunities I want, because he really wants me to be, I don't know maybe like his wife." He's very traditional in certain ways, creative in others.

At the time, Keri had two children under age 10. She had been approached by several other male colleagues about opening a new firm: "At that point, what did I have to lose? It was much less risky for me because I had a husband with a good job and I could always go back to doing technical work." After running the company for almost 10 years, Keri and her partners sold the firm. Within the past year, she and another partner opened up another company. Keri attributes her decision to become an entrepreneur to the limited career opportunities available to her due to sexism in the workplace.

Another woman stated that pay inequity prompted her business ownership. Thirty-year-old Jody Wood began her business in 1995 after it became apparent that her real estate salary was less than her male counterparts' in the same firm.

> A: I wanted to be able to make more money. I was in commercial real estate and I found that the men in my company were making more and they had the same experience.
>
> Q: How did you know this?
>
> A: They were my friends and we talked about it openly. And I know they were, and so that really bothered me, trying to fight that, so I decided that if I went out on my own, that I'd have full control which has good and bad points. . . . Sometimes I make good money and others I don't, but at least I have flexibility and I also thought that if I ever wanted to have kids I could stay home, and set my own schedule and work around that.

The decision to start a business came from feelings of being treated unfairly and unequally in the workplace. Jody, who plans to be married next year, also speaks of the added benefit of flexibility that may enable her to balance career and family responsibilities.

Lastly, one woman emphasized an incident related to sexual harassment against a fellow co-worker that prompted her to leave the company and open a business. Debbie Raymond had worked in a senior position in a large financial firm before establishing her own business in 1995.

> I left there. My emotional health didn't allow me to stay there. The vice president, the senior vice president, was sexually harassing a woman below him who came to me and reported it. There was no way to protect the company legally without going to his supervisors, who he was buddy buddy with, and it was like, "I am sorry, slap my hand." It didn't matter that he had done it before.

Debbie argues that she felt punished for continuing to push for a more severe reprimand.

> They were pressuring me to try and make it seem like, "You're not living up to your potential, we are going to fire you." And I walked around the next month totally in stress, and I finally came to the conclusion that I couldn't stand it. And I left. It was just amazing because the day after my last day with them I could breathe again.

Recent studies on women managers suggest that some women react to gendered blocks to corporate advancement by becoming entrepreneurs (Moore and Buttner 1997; Rosener 1995). Moore and Buttner (1997) find that some women become business owners due to unfriendly corporate culture, barriers, and discrimination. About one in every five of the entrepreneurs in their study left their previous corporate jobs due to dissatisfaction with the corporate good old boy system. But Moore and Buttner (1997) also suggest that discrimination is less important to departure decisions compared to other organizational and personal factors. My study confirms that, while discrimination plays a role in some women's decisions to become entrepreneurs (particularly women from upper management and professional positions), overall family-related and bureaucratic structural reasons were more commonly mentioned for entrepreneurship.

To summarize, 8 percent of the women entrepreneurs in this study established businesses to escape from gender discrimination in the workplace. All seven of these women were white, and five had previously held high-status managerial or professional jobs with relatively high levels of reward. These women emphasized the isolation they felt from male-dominated social networks, pay inequity, and sexual harassment.

RIGHT TIMING AND OPPORTUNITY

For six women in this study, business ownership resulted from being given an opportunity to establish a business that they felt they couldn't pass up. In their study of 400 women owner-managers of businesses in Quebec, Lee-Gosselin and Grise (1990) find that an even higher percentage of women became business owners by taking advantage of an existing opportunity. For one fifth of their sample, the idea to start a business originated by recognizing and seizing an opportunity.

The six women in my study characterized their decision to establish a business as "being in the right place at the right time," "the right time in my career," and "a good career move."

The experiences of Andi Costello are similar to other women who described their entrepreneurship as arising from the right timing and opportunity. Forty-year-old Andi started her interior design company in 1985.

> A: It was one of those things that fell into my lap. I just left one business and started at another company. One client called and asked me to do some work for them. I said, "We would be happy." They said, "No. We would be interested in you as a freelancer." It was an opportunity to go out on my own and I took it. I guess the opportunity came and it was a difficult decision from the standpoint of security, but I felt like I needed to take advantage of it. I always felt like I would have my own business.
>
> Q: Where do you think that feeling comes from?
>
> A: I think some of it came from looking at my father. He was a business owner, an entrepreneur. And I tend to like to have control over my own situation. I like to see the direct result of my influence. And I like flexibility. I can make as little or as much as I want. I am the point of responsibility. I have to take on that responsibility.

Like other women in this book, Andi points to the influence of an entrepreneurial family member in shaping the desire for business ownership. Andi describes the process of becoming an entrepreneur as something that just fell into her lap, but a difficult decision from the standpoint of security. And while she champions the flexibility of business ownership, she also acknowledges that the all-nighters she spent on business were not the best thing for her marriage which shortly ended in divorce.

Like Andi, 53-year-old Vicki Torres recalls growing up in an entrepreneurial family in New Mexico. Her parents were involved in a number of small, informal business endeavors.

There were seven kids in my family, so we were always trying to bring in extra money to the household income. We started selling balloons in some shopping centers and parades, and he [my father] actually would get the kids involved, so even though my father was selling balloons, he sent us kids into a parade selling balloons. So at a very early age, we were dealing with people, learning how to communicate with people, learning how to give change, learning how to sell, learning what the value of money was. So this pattern, we were always a working family, the stand where you sell novelties, the cotton candy, the hot dogs, the whole bit.

Vicki describes her family as a working family because every member contributed to the household income. After graduating from high school, Vicki married a salesman whose company moved them to several different cities in the Southwest United States. Throughout her four-year marriage, Vicki did clerical work for extra income. After her divorce, Vicki moved to San Diego in the late 1970s and did bookkeeping at a local electrical company. It was there that Vicki met Dan Braverman. Dan was starting a business of his own with another partner and they were looking for a bookkeeper. "I had set up the books here in the beginning," Vicki says, "I set up all the books, set up the procedures." In 1984, Dan's partner wanted to sell his part of the business and Dan gave Vicki the opportunity to buy into the company. In order to buy the partner out, Vicki, then single without children, turned to her family. "I borrowed money from two of my brothers, my dad, and my sister." Vicki's family acted as an important source of social and economic capital for her as an entrepreneur. Her experiences in a "working" family were important in shaping her decision to become a business owner herself. Individual family members also allowed her to carry out her ownership plans by loaning her money.

Marie Lopez also was approached by a potential business partner concerning a new company. Marie, now 33 years old, earned a bachelors degree in political science and was working in local politics when she met Victor.

He always had the idea of starting a publication that was for professional Latinos, like a general interest magazine. He had approached me once before but I wasn't ready. I liked what I was doing. But finally, after three years, I was ready to move on. We sat down and discussed what kind of magazine we wanted to do and started to piece it together.

Marie and Victor have been business partners since 1996. Still close to her dad and brothers, Marie finds that her decision to become a business owner was met with mixed emotion.

My dad was pretty supportive, but I could tell he was a little worried. I had a good job with benefits, stability. But I think he thought, "Well she's going to do what she's going to do. So rather than stress her out more or bug her. . . ." He was pretty supportive. My parents have always encouraged me to do just whatever I was happy at. My mom died about five years ago. Even before, they pushed me to go to school, finish college. In the Latino community, family is very important. The tradition is you get married, have kids, and stay home and raise the kids. My parents never did that. They always encouraged me to buy your own car, go out and travel, because you never know.

Marie's pathway to business ownership differs radically from those women who chose entrepreneurship in order to have more flexibility at home with their children. For Marie, business ownership represents a further step away from the traditional role which she describes as getting married, having children, and staying at home. Still single, Marie plans to continue to grow the business and expand into Mexican markets in the near future.

To conclude, 7 percent of the women stated that they had established their own businesses because of the right timing and opportunity. A higher proportion of Latina compared to white women started a business for this reason (14 and 5 percent, respectively). These women characterize the decision to become an entrepreneur as being in the right place at the right time.

CONCLUSION

The women entrepreneurs in this book have varied employment histories. The majority had most recently held full-time positions in the labor market, some in sales positions, others in management or service-related occupations. Why, after having been a wage or salary employee, did these women turn to business ownership? I point to five main reasons why women become entrepreneurs and establish businesses for themselves. This research suggests that Latina women appear to have a different trajectory to entrepreneurship than white women.

The most cited reason for entrepreneurship was responding to family-related concerns, such as starting home-based businesses to have flexibility for young children, establishing a partnership with a family member, or beginning a business for income after a divorce. In this study, Latinas were more likely than white women to establish businesses due to family-related concerns. A large portion of women also established businesses because of the desire for freedom from the confines of larger bureaucratic work organizations. White women were much more likely than Latinas to start businesses in response to inflexible bureaucracies. There is some statistical relationship between ethnicity and leaving the iron cage of bureaucracy for entrepreneurship. Lastly, other important pathways to business ownership included being laid off, reacting to gender discrimination at work, and having the right timing and opportunity. More Latinas than white women became entrepreneurs after having been laid off.

Women's business ownership decisions emerge in the context of the double role of women in production and reproduction relations. For some women, production in the home, in the form of a home-based business venture, means contributing to the household income while attending to reproductive domestic activities—those geared toward the continued existence of people through bearing and raising children, passing on culture, and replenishing labor power (Den Uyl 1995). Take for example, the experiences of Samantha Hatch who found that being a mother of two young children and paid worker in the labor market posed difficult challenges. She started her home-based business as a way to reconcile work and family responsibilities. This strategy, however, actually added to her workload as she struggled to maintain a profitable business and meet the needs of her children and husband. Her experiences are similar to over a dozen other women in this study.

For other women, however, entrepreneurship signals active participation in production relations and a subsequent diminishing of production and reproduction in the home. Such is the case for Andi Costello, who found that her all-nighters at the office led to her husband's increased share of the household chores. Likewise, Laura O'Neil found herself consumed by her business, spending after working hours on various client projects. Rather than engage in household labor herself, Laura paid others to do these activities—often ordering takeout and hiring a cleaning service for her home. And, as Eva Cruz increased her attention toward her party planning business, she also decreased her household responsibilities by hiring a live-in domestic worker.

I have illustrated the various pathways that women take to entrepreneurship. But how do these individual women actually go about establishing their businesses? Who offers them advice, support, or start-up money? How might these sources of capital differ between white and Latina women? These important questions are addressed in the following chapter.

CHAPTER 4

Capital and Entrepreneurship: Incorporating Gender and Ethnicity

Entrepreneurs must locate the resources or capital necessary to start and maintain successful businesses. But where do they find these resources? This chapter details the answers to these questions by incorporating Pierre Bourdieu's framework of economic, social, and cultural capital into an analysis of women's entrepreneurship.

WHERE DID YOU GET THE MONEY?

Much entrepreneurial literature is concerned with economic capital—where business owners acquire start-up or expansion capital or the amount of receipts grossed annually. Economic capital can be defined as resources that are directly convertible into money and that may be institutionalized in the form of property rights (Bourdieu 1986). For entrepreneurs, obtaining economic capital is crucial for business ownership start-up, development, and expansion.

Our access to economic capital is intricately linked to our place within the social stratification system. A typical listing of class divisions in the United States often includes the upper class, middle class, working class, and lower class. The upper class signifies families and individuals high in property ownership, wealth, bureaucratic authority, and occupational position. This class, a minute percentage of the nation, tends to have unity derived from shared educational experiences, intermarriage, and club membership. The middle class includes those with some property and high to middle occupational positions. This class is often subdivided into the upper middle class, characterized by upper-level managerial or professional positions and high educational attainment, and the lower middle class, including semiprofessionals, office workers, and salespeople. The working class encompasses lower-level, blue-collar and service workers. This class has somewhat below national average household incomes and is potentially vulnerable to financial problems. The lower class includes a diverse collection of individuals and families with little or no accumulated wealth and limited connection to the labor force. Many members of the lower class live below the government calculated poverty line, which was about $16,300 for a family of four in 1997. Over 35 million Americans, or 13 percent of the nation, lived in poverty in 1997.

I assessed the social class with which the women in this book identified. Without offering them detailed descriptions of the social classes, I asked these women which social class they felt they belonged to: the upper class, the working class, the middle class, or the lower class. All of the women identified themselves as middle class, except for five who viewed themselves as working class. Three white and two Latina women identified with the working class. Class identification research suggests that most Americans do indeed place themselves into either working or middle class categories.

I found that all of the women who used personal savings and credit, the majority of the women (83 percent), identified themselves as middle class, and confirmed the importance of having access to the financial resources necessary to get the business started.

Women in the United States who do not have personal savings or other assets, such as working class and poor women, face a significant barrier to becoming entrepreneurs, unless they can generate start-up capital from other sources, like family members or formal lending institutions. The women who identified themselves as working class were among those who borrowed money from family members for business start-up. They were fortunate that their family members had enough saved to assist them. Still, as I shall illustrate, borrowing money from family members is limited depending on the amount of their disposable income, and acquiring a loan from formal lending institutions is difficult for the majority of new business owners, especially those with working class credentials. This means that most women in this study were able to become small capitalists due to their middle class position characterized by relatively stable incomes and employment histories, high educational attainment, and accumulation of assets like a family home.

Personal Savings and Credit Most women used their own personal savings or credit as their primary financial source when starting their businesses. A higher percentage of white than Latina women used such resources (Table 4.1). Considering that most of the women's businesses are sole proprietorships in the services, start-up costs associated with such businesses tend to be relatively minimal compared to other kinds of businesses, such as manufacturing or construction. On average these women spent from $2,000 to $5,000 on business start-up costs.

Table 4.1 Primary Source of Start-Up Money by Ethnicity in My Study, 1997

Source	Ethnicity		
	White (N=67)	Latina (N=22)	Total (N=89)
Percentage Distribution			
Personal Savings and Credit Phi coefficient 0. 16	86. 6	72. 7	83. 1
Family Outside Household Phi coefficient 0. 13	9. 0	18. 2	11. 2
Formal Lending Phi coefficient 0. 09	4. 5	9. 1	5. 6

Note: Fisher's exact test was not statistically significant for these relationships.

These 74 women used a combination of cash and credit for their start-up expenses, which often included computers and software, office supplies, and furniture. Stephanie Ray, who has owned a computer consulting business since 1994, recalls, "I used my savings and I took out some lines of credit. At first I was robbing Peter to pay Paul, but now I have my credit cards balanced." Dina Berst also used a combination of savings and credit to start her health care consulting business this past year. Dina explains, "I already had a computer, equipment, and lots of supplies. But I spent about $1,000 in savings and another $4,000 on my credit card."

The National Foundation of Women Business Owners estimates that about 23 percent of women nationwide used credit cards to fund business expansions in 1999 compared with just 15 percent of men.

Over half of the women in this study began their businesses in their homes. Of the 47 women who began home-based businesses, 96 percent used their own savings. These women all championed the cost-saving benefit of operating a home-based business. Typical comments included: "I started as a home office so it didn't take a lot of start-up capital." and "I was initially homebased. This saves on the overhead."

Ten of these 47 women have moved their businesses out of their homes into office buildings. This was the case with Margaret James, who established her management consulting business at home to keep costs down. "I used savings for initial requirements and I have invested quite a lot," explains James, who has been in business for herself since 1987.

Once I had exceeded the capacity of my study, between written materials and office equipment, I had to expand. So I took over the guest room too. I had no choice. At that point my greatest limitation was space. Then my husband mentioned going out of the house. I work seven days a week, all hours, so I knew it would be hard to work out of the house, but I was able to find office space close by.

As I mentioned in Chapter 3, one-fourth of the women who were laid off (five of 20) used money from severances for business start-up. Forty-four-year-old Susan Freeman, a wedding coordinator, was offered a generous severance package consisting of one year's salary that she used to start her business in 1991. Jill Copeland, age 50, describes her severance package as the parachute from her other job that allowed her to establish a private psychotherapy practice in 1990. Likewise, Betty Simon was laid off from a large technical firm and used her severance pay to cover a substantial portion of the start-up costs, including computer equipment and furnishings. All of the other laid-off women used personal savings and credit to cover start-up costs, except for Patty Rogers who turned to her mother for economic capital.

Capital from Family Outside the Household Whereas most women started their businesses by using personal savings or credit, 11 percent primarily turned to family members outside their immediate household for start-up capital. The Small Business Administration recognizes this important source of funding, estimating that about one out of 10 women borrows money from acquaintances to start their businesses or finance expansion plans.

When talking about economic capital received from family, we need to develop more fully the concept of social capital, those valuable resources in the form of social connections of acquaintance, mutual trust, and recognition (Bourdieu 1984, 1986). Bourdieu (1986) characterizes social capital as a durable network of relationships.

> These relationships may exist only in the practical state, in material and/or symbolic exchanges which help to maintain them. They may also be socially instituted and guaranteed by the application of a common name (the name of a family, a class, or a tribe or of a school, a party, etc.) and by a whole set of instituting acts designed simultaneously to form and inform those who undergo them; in this case, they are more or less really enacted and so maintained and reinforced, in exchanges (Bourdieu 1986:249).

According to Bourdieu (1986), one's network of connections is not a natural given but the product of investment strategies designed to reproduce useful relationships that can secure material or symbolic profits.

Family relationships can act as useful forms of social capital. Probably every American can point to some time in their lives when they were assisted by immediate family members or extended kin. Throughout our lives, we often rely on family for emotional, spiritual, and financial support. Social network research suggests that racial and ethnic minorities in the U.S., in particular African Americans and Latinos, are more likely than white Americans to rely on extended kinship networks for various social supports (Hays and Mindel 1973; Wagner and Schaffer 1980). Explanations for familialism among minority families have ranged from cultural to structural. Some research suggests that cultural norms and values of minority groups underscore the importance of ties to a larger kin group (Wagner and Schaffer 1980). Other research contends that limited economic resources cause minority families to be more familiastic (Baca Zinn 1989). Recent research, however, suggests a decline in network participation and informal social support among minority families (Roschelle 1997; Wilson 1987). Using national survey data to examine participation in extended social support networks, Anne Roschelle (1997) finds that Anglo men and women actually give to and receive from network members more child care and household assistance than African Americans, Chicanos, and Puerto Ricans. Challenging the theory that familialism may result from economic deprivation, Roschelle's study also indicates that as one's socioeconomic status increases, so does the likelihood of his or her participation in extended support networks.

How might familialism relate to an entrepreneur's search for economic capital for new business ventures? Studies examining self-employment among immigrants in the United States find that the family is often a crucial source of economic support for the establishment and operation of immigrant-owned small businesses. Sanders and Nee (1996) argue that immigrants often approach members of their extended family for financial assistance before seeking business partners outside the family. Such a preference appears to reflect pragmatic concerns of the potential for conflict and increased transaction costs when nonfamily business partners are involved (Sanders and Nee 1996).

For some women, family members act as a crucial form of social capital by initially investing in their entrepreneurial endeavors. Ten women in this study relied on the economic contribution of parents or siblings for business start-up capital. A higher percentage of Latina than white women used family sources (18 and 9 percent, respectively; Phi coefficient=.13; Fisher's exact test not significant: p=0.26).

As mentioned in Chapter 1, 41-year-old Patty Rogers was able to open her accounting business thanks to the financial support of her mother. Growing up, Patty witnessed her mom, who was widowed, working at a number of small businesses, including specialty cleaning. Patty recalls having her first job when she was a teenager. "At that time, I bought all my own shoes, and by high school I was buying my own clothes too," Patty explains.

When she first established her business in 1994, Patty turned to her mother for the money necessary to establish the business. Her husband Frank's salary supports their lifestyle, but could not generate the capital Patty needed to start the business. She borrowed money from her mother and paid her back at fair market rate. Over the last three years, she has borrowed a total of $12,000. Patty currently owes her mother about $1,000. The money Patty has borrowed has allowed her to set up a home office with furniture, file cabinets, and a computer system.

After graduating from art school, 39-year-old Cindy Kelley turned to her family for financial assistance when she decided to open an art studio and gallery. Her uncle, also an artist, initially rented the studio space with her. Cindy relied on money from her sister and mother too. When I asked if she had considered taking out a formal loan, Cindy (who has never been married) responded, "No because it's a lot harder for a single woman to get a loan. My mother had tried to get a large loan in the mid 1970s, but she couldn't get one because she didn't have a man co-sign." From an early age, Cindy assisted her mother in her photography business. Today, Cindy often turns to her mother for business advice as well as financial support.

Likewise, 56-year-old Christine Myers relied on money from her parents in order to establish her credit information and financial services company. Christine had grown up in an entrepreneurial family. Her parents established a collection services business when she was young. Christine recalls,

> I had no idea what I wanted to be when I grew up. My sister was on her way to becoming an artist, but I knew that wasn't for me. I began hanging out in my mother's and dad's office more. The machinery interested me, and the people they dealt with, negotiated with. They knew about everyone's business. They were in collections. It changed continually. It was never boring and I decided that this kind of work was what I wanted to go into.

After taking some university courses in business administration, Christine went to work for her parents in the collection agency. Shortly after, Christine was married and moved to Arizona with her husband, Rick. After her divorce over 10 years ago, Christine returned to Southern California. She took over the family business in 1986 and has managed its daily operations ever since. She relied on her parents, then in their 70s, for a small loan in order to expand the business. She continues to consult them when making important business decisions. I asked Christine if she had ever turned to a formal institution for a loan. She responded:

> Trying to get a loan is demeaning. When I was married it was no problem, but now it's more difficult. I finally got local banks to give me a line of credit. But mostly I've gotten no help. I couldn't go to the SBA [Small Business

Administration] because they won't secure a loan if you haven't posted a profit for three years prior to the loan.

Vicki Torres and Marie Lopez are two Latinas in this book who turned to family members for economic assistance. Vicki was given the opportunity to buy half of a company by her acquaintance Dan Braverman. In order to buy out Dan's business partner, Vicki turned to her brothers, dad, and sister. "No formal loan, just family. And I knew I could pay them back. I just needed the money quick, right then," Vicki explains. Considering that Vicki grew up in a family in which the children were integrated with income-generating activities—selling balloons, novelties, and fireworks—Vicki correctly assumed that her brothers, sisters, and father would be willing to assist with her business venture.

Marie Lopez was approached by potential business partner, Victor, about establishing a new publication that targeted the Hispanic market. In order to start up the company, Marie took out a loan with her father, who lives a few doors down from her in the same neighborhood. For Marie, her father represented a more realistic source of capital than a formal lending institution.

Banks are reluctant to make loans to businesses like publications. They were willing to look at established businesses. But it's not as easy as people make it out to be to get a business loan. We'd like to bring in some more equipment, and we'll have a more solid track record soon to expand.

An interesting trend emerges among those women who turned to family members for business start-up funds. As children growing up, these women tended to be involved in productive activities that contributed somehow to the family income. Vicki Torres sold novelties or fireworks with her brothers and sisters, Cindy Kelley assisted her mother's photography business, Christine Myers eventually worked in her parent's collections agency, and Patty Rogers used the income from part-time jobs to buy shoes and clothes in high school. This relationship of production shared by children and parents seemed to prompt the women to feel they could turn to family for economic assistance as adults. Other sources could have been used, such as credit card debt, second mortgages, or equipment rentals instead of purchases. Yet these women, Latina and white, chose family sources over these other options. Their families trusted them based on prior business dealings and exchanges.

A Bank Loan The literature on entrepreneurship finds that acquiring adequate economic capital, especially from formal lending institutions, is a greater obstacle for women than men entrepreneurs (Bender 1978; Goffee and Scase 1985; Hisrich 1989; Hisrich and O'Brien 1981; Pellegrino and Reece 1982; Schwartz 1976; Van der Wees and Romijn 1995). Lee-Gosselin's and

Grise's (1990) study of 400 women owner-managers of businesses in Quebec finds that the most frequent obstacles encountered when establishing a business are lack of confidence shown by banks, suppliers and clients (33 percent). Many of these women (38 percent) thought these obstacles were related to their gender (Lee-Gosselin and Grise 1990). Van der Wees and Romijin (1995) suggest that women entrepreneurs may encounter problems in the financial arena because of the size and nature of their businesses. Women's businesses are often very small and financial institutions may consider their small loans unprofitable. Hisrich (1989) argues that women entrepreneurs have difficulties in dealing with lending institutions because many lack financial track records in business or management experience. This was, in fact, a frequent complaint of the women in this study. They stated that because they hadn't been in business long enough, business loans were inaccessible to them.[1]

Very few women in this book, three white and two Latina, turned to formal lending institutions for start-up capital. All of these women were married at the time of starting a business. Their businesses tend to be atypical of most in this book: they all have employees, gross revenues well over $100,000 annually, and have always existed outside the home. Claudia Sanchez is one Latina woman who secured a bank loan. Claudia has extensive educational credentials, including a bachelors and a masters degree in science and a masters degree in business administration. In 1991, Claudia and her husband Ricardo established their company. When I asked Claudia where they got the money to start the business, she responded, "That's a very big part of the story right there. That's the make or break point, if you don't have your own start-up capital." Claudia and Ricardo had some money to invest in the company, but needed an additional $100,000.

> We put together a list of everyone that we could think of. I mean, everyone who might be interested in this kind of a start-up. We included some foundations and associations, professional organizations involved with helping women in business, small businesses, whatever. We just thought we'd tap every place that we could think of to try to get some capital.

Claudia and Ricardo tried for months to raise the funds, but were turned down by dozens of possible funding sources. She describes the process of trying to find funding as "very, very difficult" and "one of the toughest things that we had to do." At this point, thinking that they might never get the money, Ricardo secured other employment.

> So he had gone back to work, you know, we were really having to start to think that if this doesn't work, we're going to have to go on and do something else.

And in the last possible hour, we had offers from two banks, not just one, two banks. This was after, of course, presentations where you go in and present your business plan and, you know, meet the bank committee, lending officer and so on. So we were able to choose between the two. And so we ended up with a $100,000 loan, SBA guaranteed bank loan.

Claudia recognizes the significance of one person in particular, lending officer Sara Michaels, in securing the bank loan. Michaels oversaw the loan process, and when she recently moved to another bank, Claudia and Ricardo transferred their account with her. "This woman is so valued to us," Claudia explains, "She sees a successful plan and she believes in it and in the people. She backs them and supports them with the resources that she has as well as moral support." Currently, Claudia and Ricardo have two employees (the business, which is incorporated, technically has four employees including Claudia and Ricardo). Their company grosses about $500,000 annually.

Anita Jordon had a different experience when searching for funding for her business. Born in Mexico, Anita and her parents and siblings moved to the United States when she was age 7. Anita describes her father as "a business man who did very well in Mexico, but didn't like the lifestyle there." Her father started a bookstore in San Diego and Anita's mother stayed home and cared for the family. After earning an associate's degree at a local community college, Anita worked as a secretary. Knowing that Anita wanted to quit her job, her father offered her a job in the bookstore. Anita was married in 1989, and shortly after, her father offered to sell them the bookstore.

I had managed the store. I had worked there and about a year down the line, he offered it to us to buy and I bought it from him. It's a partnership with my husband, but he doesn't work here. He's a manager at a grocery store. I run the bookstore.

She recalls the relative ease with which they secured the money to buy the bookstore. The bookstore was not technically a start-up venture as in the case of Claudia and Ricardo. It had been run profitably for a number of years. "We had to take out a loan," says Anita, "It wasn't bad because first we got it through a private lender and then used home equity as a security." What is interesting to me about Anita's account of buying the store is her use of "us" and "I" in talking about purchasing the business. Anita was clear that her father offered the bookstore to "us," her and her husband, yet is equally clear that "I" manage and run it.

Anita's bookstore grosses about $200,000 annually. She would like to increase revenues by about 20 percent each year. Now age 29 with a small child,

Anita continues to work in the bookstore full-time and has three part-time employees.

Dawn Nelson, age 35, also bought an existing business by taking out a loan. After working for more than five years at a small, copy center, Dawn had the opportunity to buy the business from the existing owner. Dawn's husband, a military officer, offered moral support, but their savings were not enough to cover the costs of buying the business. Still, Dawn was able to secure financing fairly easily. She describes the process of securing the bank loan as a "whirlwind process, pretty quick. The previous owner really wanted to sell. I basically went through the process thinking, gee okay, I guess. Not really knowing what it was all about." Dawn found that the previous owner was most helpful in offering advice on the business and financial side. A sole proprietor, Dawn currently employs four people. Her gross revenues range between $200,000 and $500,000 annually.[2]

In sum, most women used personal savings or credit as their primary financial source when starting their businesses. A higher percentage of white than Latina women used these resources. Eleven percent relied on the economic contribution of parents or siblings for business start-up capital. A slightly higher percentage of Latina than white women used family sources. Very few women turned to formal lending institutions for start-up capital.

WHO ADVISES YOU?

I have discussed the concept of social capital when examining the economic assistance provided by family members to some of the women entrepreneurs. I will now turn to other social relationships and connections that offer crucial advice or assistance to these women.

Entrepreneurs are embedded in a social context, facilitated or inhibited by their position in social networks that can be crucial for business success (Aldrich 1989; Aldrich et al 1995). As with all forms of capital, social capital depends on norms of inclusion and exclusion that often relate to ethnicity, race, gender, national background, and social class (Fernandez-Kelly 1994). More frequently, people in business with high economic and cultural capital travel in social circles distant from those without such capital. This division often coincides with gender, racial, and ethnic inequalities.

Some studies suggest that men and women entrepreneurs are embedded in different social relations and networks. One theory of gender differences in networking argues that women use different channels to seek business assistance and view business activity as holistically integrated into the rest of their lives. Brush (1992) contends that women's business relationships are more integrated with family and personal relationships; therefore, women may be less comfortable contacting strangers and more likely to turn to family and friends than work associates for advice and assistance.

These findings, however, contradict a recent study by Aldrich et al (1995) that reveals women's networking is only marginally different from men's, with the main difference being that women are more likely to turn to other women for some of the assistance they need. Their interview data from over 200 men and women entrepreneurs in North Carolina find that, whereas men entrepreneurs turn overwhelmingly to other men for assistance, women also turn mostly to men, although not to the same extent as male owners. Aldrich et al (1995) also find that men and women entrepreneurs use similar channels, such as friends and business associates, when seeking legal or financial business assistance and receive similarly high-quality assistance. In contrast to Brush's conclusions, they contend that women entrepreneurs do not show greater inclination than men entrepreneurs to ask family for help. An earlier study by Pat Ray Reese (1993) also suggests that women entrepreneurs' resource contacts are no different than their male counterparts'. Reese's analysis of 444 questionnaires and 353 telephone interviews suggests that men and women entrepreneurs know the same number of resource people, such as lawyers, accountants, loan officers and suppliers, and do not differ in their use of these resources.

From these network studies, it appears that women and men entrepreneurs use similar weak-network channels in seeking out financial or legal assistance, but research finds that women tend to be left out of strong-tie business networks that provide men entrepreneurs access to diverse economic and cultural resources needed for business survival (Adrich et al 1989). The question remains, who comprises women entrepreneurs' strong-tie networks? Who might regularly assist and advise these women?

In this study, I equate strong-tie business relationships with the concept of mentoring. Mentors are important forms of social capital because a mentoring relationship is characterized by one individual acting as a trusted counselor or teacher to another. I asked the women in this study if they had any mentors, individuals whose advice or assistance they have relied upon regularly during their time as business owners. Over 40 percent of the women did not characterize themselves as having a mentor in business (Table 4.2). Keri Slater, who owns a consulting business, notes, "I don't have any mentors. There are no mentors, somebody looking after my own good. The last one was my math teacher in high school. But I think there are people who give support in different ways." The women who described themselves without mentorship emphasized that they were doing it on their own, learning from life experience, and relying on trial and error. The remaining 52 women identified one or several mentors who had offered them some kind of business assistance or advice throughout the years. I asked these women to characterize their relationship to their mentor(s).

This resulted in a total of 62 responses (Table 4.3). Of those women who have mentors, over half identified mentors within their industry. This was the case with Gloria Morales who established a personnel agency after being laid off in 1994.

Table 4.2 Mentorship in My Study by Ethnicity, 1997.

Mentorship	White (N=67)	Latina (N=22)	Total Sample (N=89)
Percentage Distribution			
No Mentor	37. 3	54. 5	41. 6 (37)
Mentor	62. 7	45. 5	58. 4 (52)
Phi coefficient 0. 15			

Note: Fisher's exact test was not statistically significant: p=0. 21.

Table 4.3 Relationship of Mentor to Each Woman Entrepreneur in My Study, 1997.

Mentor Responses	White Responses (N=52)	Latina Responses (N=10)	Total (N=62)
Percentage Distribution			
Mentors in Same Industry	57. 7	40. 0	54. 8 (34)
Family Members as Mentors	26. 9	0. 0	22. 6 (14)
Bankers, Accountants, Lawyers	7. 7	40. 0	12. 9 (8)
Clients as Mentors	7. 7	20. 0	9. 7 (6)

Note: A total of 52 women in the study identified themselves as having a mentor. Of these women, some identified mentors in more than one category, therefore there are more responses here.

> You know, surprisingly enough I turned to my former boss. You know, he took me under his wing and said, "If you ever need me for anything give me a call." My thinking was, I didn't expect to. But when I started the business, he offered me advice. I'd call and ask him, "Who would you go to? What about mark ups?" Sometimes he's helpful and sometimes he doesn't really give me the information, but he is the one person that I really kind of turn to.

Gloria continues to rely on her former boss' input when she is unsure of business dealings and practices. Samantha Hatch, owner of a training and development company, also relies on mentorship from another person in her industry.

I actively seek mentors. I have one right now, a guy who has 10 years experience. He's a consultant who is very successful and we get together about once a month. We have lunch meetings and we'll do e-mails. I met him through one of the organizational meetings. I've always had mentors though.

Likewise, public relations business owner Maggie Snow recalls who she turned to when she first opened her agency.

You know, this is funny. People that I thought that I could go to for advice, I really didn't get much advice from and people that I wasn't even thinking about just kind of came out. There hasn't been a whole lot of support, but there is one woman. She owns an agency here in town. So I'll call her and ask, "Look, I'm faced with this situation, what's your professional advice?"

Fewer women named business professionals, such as accountants, lawyers, and bankers, and clients as sources of mentorship.

Unlike Brush's (1992) contention that women business owners rely heavily on family for advice and assistance, only 14 women view family members as business mentors (23 percent of those with mentors). These women all turned to family members who had experience as entrepreneurs themselves.

Ten of these women relied on parents who had worked for some portion of their careers as small business owners. Laura O'Neil, for instance, characterizes her entrepreneurial father as a source of mentorship.

My Dad, he won't give advice if I don't solicit it from him and when I do, his advice kind of comes in parables. . . . I look to him like in times of, "Oh my God, where is my next client coming from?" In times like that, I look at him and the business that he's built and know that he has gone through the same thing and I find comfort in that, because I know one year he had to sell the car to pay the tax bill. I know he's been through tough times and I know he made it through. I know I'm not alone.

Christine Myers also named her father and mother as her business mentors. Christine took over and expanded the family collection services business in 1986. She explains that, for a brief time, her parents actually came back and worked for her. Christine describes them as her mainstay.

Four other women, who all began partnerships with their husbands, named their husbands as business mentors. Anna Espinoza was one of these women. She opened an architecture firm in 1994.

My husband, he's also an architect. We had talked about opening our own firm. Originally our plan was to have a firm together and work together. After the first year, it didn't work out that way. He became less involved, but I still bounce ideas off of him and ask for his opinions about clients.

Even though they are no longer business partners and Anna runs the business by herself, the process of starting the business together allows Anna to feel as though her husband can still provide valuable business advice and assistance.

Table 4.4 Mentors by Sex According to the Women in My Study, 1997

Source	Total Women with Mentors (N=52)
Percentage Distribution	
Women Mentors Only	23. 1
Men Mentors Only	38. 5
Men and Women Mentors	38. 5

Another significant point raised by the networking literature suggests a gender bias in the composition of women's networks. Aldrich and Sakano (1998) find that women entrepreneurs' advisor circles of strong-tie relationships have a different gender composition than men's. While few men include women in their advisor circles, women entrepreneurs are involved in mainly cross-sex networks, dealing with mostly men but also a high proportion of women (Aldrich and Sakano 1998). My study finds that women entrepreneurs primarily rely on mentors who are men (39 percent) or both men and women mentors (39 percent). Less than one fourth of the women with mentors named only other women as sources of mentorship. This trend has much to do with the gender composition of the labor market. Most of the women relied on mentors who already had established careers in the same industry. It makes sense that a large number of these individuals are men, considering that structural constraints in the workplace and family considerations have historically limited women's access to jobs and skills that would enable women to mentor other business owners. These constraints have been lessened through anti-discrimination policies, changing gender roles, and women's higher educational attainment. However, compared to women, men still overwhelmingly hold high-paying positions with high authority and advancement potential, the kinds of positions that individuals could use to effectively mentor entrepreneurs.

I also was curious about how women entrepreneurs might use their membership in professional or social organizations to assist their businesses. In particular I wanted to assess a little researched question: What are the possible benefits of all-women business networking organizations for women entrepreneurs? In recent years there has been tremendous growth in all-women's professional and business organizations. To what degree do such groups provide assistance to women entrepreneurs?

Almost half of the women in this book (46 percent) had attended at least one all-women's business function at some point in their business ownership history. There is a notable variation by ethnicity in women's participation in all-women's business organizations. White women were more likely than Latina to have attended all-women's business functions (52 and 27 percent, respectively).

Of the women who had participated in all-women's businesses organizations, about two-thirds emphasized the primarily psychological advantages of such organizations.

Doris Lamont, the owner of an appraisal business, is a regular participant of one all-women business organization in town.

> You get to know people. One woman is a financial planner. I don't have a need for her services, but if I came across someone who has a need for her, I'll pass on her information. You develop a knowledge of people and what they do. It's easier for women to talk to women about how to start a business and balance out their lives between home and business. Women like to help women.

This sentiment is echoed by Kim McDonald who also believes that all-women's business organizations can be valuable: "I can see how other women have adjusted, coped with family and business."

Keri Slater belongs to two professional all-women's organizations. Keri explains the typical meeting: "You go in, you have dinner, you say, "My company's in shambles," and spend three minutes on that and then say, "But I'm really worried about my daughter or husband or our relationship."" Even though she doesn't gain concrete advice related to her business practices, Keri still attends these meetings because she finds that they offer her support and an opportunity to network with women in similar positions of power.

Shelley Johnson characterizes these benefits as emotional, but not tangible. Shelley, age 48, started her marketing consulting business in 1995. She asserts that all-women's organizations are especially important to new business owners or young women because they provide guidance and build confidence. "They are testing the waters," Shelley explains. "When you start finding that your peers are receiving you, it is a wonderful confidence booster."

While all-women business organizations appear to offer support and motivation, only 14 women have acquired information from these groups that directly benefited their company's bottom line, such as viable client leads, money-saving marketing strategies, or other business opportunities.

Accounting business owner Patty Rogers has received several referrals from all-women's networking functions.

> The referrals are only a $150 tax return or a $300 tax return but once I do them, then I do auntie May and cousin George and so there is plenty of that. The spider web grows. Because if I can get the son and daughter-in-law then I can work on the mother-in-law and then I can work on the mother-in-law's bridge friends versus if I get one good lead for a business organization, that maybe the only work I get from that. So this may come out to be $7,000 but then it doesn't go any further.

Maureen Davis, who owns a beauty business, elaborates, "I think I go [to all-women's functions] for the networking of it although I've not gotten a whole lot of clients from there. I have gotten some clients, but I don't think these groups are as good as people like to think they are."

About one third of the women who had participated in all-women's business functions did not find the psychological benefits helpful, and in fact, would have preferred more concrete advice and assistance related directly to running a business.

Samantha Hatch owns a company that designs instructional materials. She elaborates on this point of view.

> I've been to some of these [all-women's] groups and it's only the cover page that has to do with professional women. As soon as you get into it, they'd rather talk about their diet. I don't get anything out of that. I find that if men are there, then if those women want to do that they'll congregate with other women like that. I do better when there's a mix. I think it's richer when you have both [men and women].

Other women added the following comments:

> They are too expensive for what you get.

> I don't like them. The last meeting I went to, I can't describe, it was more touchy, feely. It was on communication and stress, and I guess I didn't take it seriously, and I didn't think there were any prospects for me there.

> I got away from the women organizations because our differences are just too great. I'm not doing the flower or beauty shops or things like that.

Like many of the white women, most Latina women also emphasized the drawbacks of all-women's groups, especially their expense and their touchy, feely nature.[3]

If Latina women do not benefit from all-women's business functions, do they perhaps find co-ethnic business organizations (or those specifically designed for Latina business women) more helpful for business advice and assistance? A significant shortcoming of prior networking studies on gender and entrepreneurship is their lack of attention to the impact of race and ethnicity on entrepreneurs' use of social capital. The significance of ethnicity on social networking has been raised in the literature on ethnic and immigrant entrepreneurs. Such research indicates that co-ethnic networks, such as protected ethnic markets and loyal co-ethic employees, are often crucial for business success among ethnic minorities and immigrants in the United States (Light and Bonacich 1988; Portes and Bach 1985; Waldinger 1986). When academics study immigrant or ethnic entrepreneurship, however, they often ignore the significance of gender. I address how Latina women entrepreneurs might capitalize on co-ethnic networks in the following chapter on Latina entrepreneurship.

SPOUSE AS CAPITAL

Although a small proportion of women view other family members as business mentors, family still provides an important source of support, whether financial or psychological. For married women, I was curious to know what role their spouses play in their businesses. How much influence do spouses have on the way these women run their businesses and on their business objectives?

Sixty-one percent of the women in this study are currently married. A higher proportion of Latina than white women are married (68 and 58 percent, respectively). Unlike women who have never been married, married women (and some divorced) can rely on their spouses for additional family income. Many of the women assert that their husbands' salaries provided crucial financial support and benefits to their families, especially during the first years of their businesses. The reversal of this pattern, relying on the wife's income while the husband establishes a business, often occurs too. In their study of men entrepreneurs, Scase and Goffee (1982) find that women's paid employment can be an important source of income during the initial period of their husband's business formation.

Keri Slater is one of the women who relied heavily on her husband's income. Recall that she had experienced gender discrimination in a large scientific company and decided to establish a new company after being approached by male colleagues about opening a firm. Keri explains that it was much less risky for her because she had a husband with a well-paying job. After running the company for a number of years, Keri and her partners sold the firm. Within the past year, she and another partner opened up another company. "We put in enough funds to provide furniture, computers, and our consulting contracts are going to be beginning to pay the bills," Keri explains. "We aren't taking salaries right now." Once again, Keri's husband's well-paid position as a medical doctor allowed her to establish a company without worrying about immediate income.

Currently divorced, Laura O'Neil still provides a good example of relying on her husband's income while establishing her public relations business. Laura explains that when she started her business two years ago, she was still married. "It was nice to have the support of that other income because my income went from, you know, $50,000 a year to zero pretty much," says Laura. When asked what it would have been like if she started her business without being married, Laura answers, "It wouldn't have been a snap. I would have had to start building a clientele while I was still employed full time." Her husband's salary clearly smoothed the way for her becoming a business owner. While there were other possible routes to ownership, such as working full-time and moonlighting on the business, Laura was able to devote her total energy toward her business and, within two years of opening, gross $50,000 annually.

Wendy Caulder, age 40, experienced a more difficult time establishing her business, considering that her previous salary was higher than her husband's. Wendy, who has a bachelors degree in computer science, began a computer consulting business in 1993 after feeling that there was little room for advancement at her prior place of employment. She used her savings for business start-up costs, but explains that business profits were slow coming.

> The first few years of the business, it was tough because I was the main wage earner before. He [my husband] has a great salary and benefits, but I was still the main wage earner. So the income issue has been really stressful. Now it's better because I'm in my fourth year and starting to see some income myself. But it's taken until this year to get there. Without his income, I wouldn't have lasted.

Since 1993, Wendy has hired a number of temporary and contract workers and this past year, her business grossed over $500,000. Wendy explains her desire to now stabilize her income.

> I want more projects to bill out. Before I wanted a lot of growth, now I just want a nice, comfortable business. We had a few lean years in the beginning, and now I just want regular paychecks. I don't want to be a millionaire, just regular paychecks.

An important pattern emerges among the married women in this study. One third of these married women (and one fifth of the total sample) own a business in which their husband is regularly involved. A higher proportion of married Latina compared to married white women characterize their husbands as highly integrated with business activities (47 and 23 percent, respectively).

Table 4.5 Husband Integrated in the Business by Ethnicity in My Study, 1997

	White (N =39)	Latina (N=15)	Total (N=54)
Percentage Distribution			
Married, Husband Integrated	23. 0	46. 7	29. 6
Married, Husband Not Integrated	77. 0	53. 3	70. 4
Phi coefficient=0. 23			

Note: Fisher's exact test: p<0.1.

What might explain the increased business participation of husbands of Latina women entrepreneurs? For both Latina and white women, having a husband who is in the same industry increases the likelihood that a business partnership will form. However, viewing the labor market as devoid of other employment options also acted as a catalyst to business partnership between Latina wives and husbands.

Silvia Carrillo, age 50, has owned a translation business since 1984. Born in the United States, Silvia decided to work in Mexico after earning her bachelors degree in literature. In Mexico, she taught English as a Second Language to university students. It was there that Silvia met her husband, Luis. In the early 1980s, Silvia and Luis moved back to the United States. While Luis found work as a financial consultant, Silvia decided to open a business translating materials in Spanish and English. For most of their lives, Silvia's and Luis' work experiences have been separate. However, ever since Luis was laid off four years ago, he has worked in Silvia's business. "The job prospects [for Luis] were slim in this area," Silvia comments. Silvia's translation business allowed Luis to continue working without a significant break in his career. Subsequently, Silvia's business has profited by expanding to include international clients with whom Luis deals. Heather Reyes had a similar situation in which her husband joined her management consulting business after being laid off.

Unlike Silvia and Heather, whose husbands joined their businesses, Cynthia Valdes, age 45, began working in her husband's existing business. After earning a bachelors degree in English, Cynthia took various positions in public relations writing. In 1983, Cynthia married Stephan, and shortly after, they established a home-based, contracting partnership. Originally, Stephan assumed most of the business responsibility, but Cynthia explains how she became more involved in the business.

> It was originally his realm, construction, but as time went on, the part of business that I knew best was needed, financial management. I became more involved in the everyday necessities and then became part owner. I got my general contractor license in 1993.

In contrast to Silvia's and Luis' story, Cynthia entered her husband's existing business because of family-related reasons. Cynthia and Stephan still have three young children, and running a home-based business allowed for flexibility with the kids.

For Julia Rivera, 63-years-old, the decision to enter business with her husband came after her children were grown. Julia earned a bachelors degree in business and worked in household finance until she had her first child. "They [my employers] wanted me to go back to work right away and I said, 'No,'" Julia explains, "I was even making more than my husband, but I wanted to be there for my children." Born in 1934, Julia is a member of the postwar generation of parents who raised their children during the 1950s and 1960s. During this time, according to Katherine Newman (1993), attention focused on bringing up the kids: "The target of all this concern was, of course, mother. . . . Raising children became their moral mission, their job." After her four children had grown, Julia felt that her best opportunity for employment was working with her husband, who is an engineer. She did not have a substantial career history, which she felt placed her at a disadvantage in finding employment. In 1989, Julia and her husband opened a retail business. While Julia deals with the day-to-day business activities and customer relations, her husband handles the product side of the business.

In this study, I find that Latina women entrepreneurs more often have businesses in which their husbands are integrated than white women. This has much to do with Latinas' perceptions that few other opportunities exist in the labor market. Comments included: "The job prospects were slim in this area," "He was laid off from his previous job," and "I saw the best opportunity was to start something with my husband." While three of these Latina women entered into partnerships with their husbands from the beginning, two Latina women joined their husband's firms and two women owned businesses that their husbands joined after being laid-off.

Another notable pattern emerges among the married business women. The percentage of women with dependent children is much lower for those married women whose husbands are integrated in their businesses (Table 4.6). Whereas only one fourth of women whose husbands participated in their businesses had dependent children (and 38 percent do not have children), over one third of women without husband participation had dependent children.

What is the relationship between household composition and the integration of spouses' income-generating activities? It could be that when couples have dependent children, they chose not to integrate their activities because there's more to risk when both partners are working at the same business. There is the possibility of loss of income and benefits, such as health insurance.

Table 4.6 Having Children and Husband Integrated in the Business in My Study, 1997

	Husband Integrated (N =16)	Husband Not Integrated (N=38)
Percentage Distribution		
No Children	37. 5	23. 7
Dependent Children (Under Age 18)	25. 0	34. 2
Adult Children (Age 18 and Over)	37. 5	42. 1

Mary Munoz and her husband decided to sever their business partnership once they had children. Mary offers insight when describing the start-up of her architecture firm. After earning a bachelors degree in architecture, Mary worked in several other large firms before starting her own practice. When she met her husband, also an architect, it seemed natural for them to think about a business partnership together. In 1992, they opened their own firm.

Originally our plan was to have a firm together and work together. After our first year, it didn't work out that way. He has become much less involved. I still bounce ideas off of him, but he is now at another firm. Originally it was like a fifty-fifty partnership, but now our careers are separate, even though I still have his name in our portfolio for the business as a consultant.

What happened to end the partnership? Mary explains that shortly after opening the business, she took some time off to have their first child. This meant less time and energy directed at the business.

I couldn't generate enough income to be secure. It's very depressing, but I just couldn't generate enough business. After opening the firm, I had a child. Our first child had heart complications and that has taken up a lot of my time. So we started with the business out of the home, and then he worked for another firm.

Mary continues to run the business with the assistance of two employees and some outside consultants. Her firm currently grosses between $50,000 and $100,000 annually.

Mary's case illustrates a common trend among dual income couples. Women tend to assume greater domestic and child care responsibilities that might place them in precarious organizational or work-related positions (Blau 1984; Hochschild 1989). Whereas married women tend to take more time off for family than their husbands, a practice that can give the impression of poor work commitment and may hamper advancement, often men's productive activities remain relatively uncompromised by family obligations.

But what happens when a husband and wife engage in the same productive activity, such as a business partnership? As we witness in Mary's case, increased domestic responsibilities, like having young children, ultimately influenced not only her, but also his, production negatively. While it's commonplace for dual-income couples to have children, once they do, we know that women generally curtail their work-related activities for the family. Yet when both husband and wife are business partners, it becomes apparent that having young children ultimately involves sacrificing his productive activity (as well as hers) because one of them inevitably reduces attention toward the business. This can translate into loss of clients and revenue. This is crucial in explaining why fewer married couples who are business partners have young children, and why such a high proportion of these couples have no children at all.

In sum, women entrepreneurs rely on social relationships to assist them in their business endeavors. Eleven percent of the women relied on the economic contribution of parents or siblings for business start-up capital. I asked the women if they had any mentors, individuals whose advice or assistance they have relied upon regularly during their time as business owners. Over 40 percent did not characterize themselves as having a mentor in business. Most of the women who have mentors identified mentors within their industry. A higher proportion of married Latina compared to married white women relied on their husband's contribution to their businesses.

CULTURAL CAPITAL

Resources in the form of economic and social capital are crucial for women's entrepreneurial success. Cultural capital is another significant form of capital. This concept has roots in Max Weber's conception of society's class, status, and party hierarchies. Weber viewed status as a ranking based on honor, prestige, and respect that relates to one's lifestyle, formal education, and occupation (Weber 1968). Bourdieu's (1986) concept of cultural capital underscores the significance of status.

Cultural capital can exist in three forms: in the *embodied* state, i.e., in the form of long-lasting dispositions of the mind and body; in the *objectified* state, in the form of cultural goods (pictures, books, dictionaries, instruments, machines, etc.), which are the trace or realization of theories or critiques of these theories, problematics, etc.; and in the *institutionalized* state, a form of objectification which must be set apart because, as will be seen in the case of educational qualifications, it confers entirely original properties on the cultural capital which it is presumed to guarantee (p. 243).

According to Bourdieu, cultural capital is significant because it can be used to accumulate additional social and economic advantages and yield profits of distinction for its owner (Bourdieu 1986). Bourdieu argues that cultural capital is derived from one's location in the social landscape. The more privileged one's status in that landscape, the better one's endowment of cultural capital. One's access to cultural capital relates to one's position within gender, race, and class hierarchies.

EDUCATION AS INSTITUTIONALIZED CULTURAL CAPITAL

In his discussion of institutionalized cultural capital, which includes educational qualifications, Bourdieu (1986) establishes how his concept differs from human capital theorists. Human capital theory presumes that one's economic progress is the function of supply-side characteristics such as education, experience, ability, and individual preferences. These theorists argue that characteristics of the worker, like education and experience, are more significant in determining income and mobility than ascriptive factors, such as a person's race or gender (Becker 1975). Bourdieu developed the notion of cultural capital by relating children's academic success to the distribution of cultural capital between social classes. Bourdieu (1986) argues that "this starting point implies a break with the presuppositions inherent both in the common sense view, which sees academic success or failure as an effect of natural aptitudes, and in human capital theories" (p. 243). He argues that human capital theorists do not place enough significance on the fact that scholastic ability is itself a product of an investment of cultural capital. Bourdieu establishes that the definition of human capital "does not move beyond economism and ignores, *inter alia*, the fact that the scholastic yield from educational action depends on the cultural capital previously invested by the family. Moreover, the economic and social yield of the educational qualification depends on the social capital, again inherited, which can be used to back it up" (p. 244). Family and social connections can impact access to quality education, success in school, and valued positions gained later in life.

The extent of our educational attainment and credentials, forms of institutionalized cultural capital, impact our position within the occupational structure. We know that the professions, such as law, medicine, and architecture, enjoy high income and prestige. Individuals entering such professions need to attain advanced educational and professional credentials. It also is clear that attainment of advanced degrees, such as masters in business administration, can increase the likelihood of reaching top managerial positions in corporate America. The link between educational attainment and occupational position translates into differences in income for different levels of schooling. College attendance generally promises higher income. In 1993, women with a high school degree typically earned about $10,900; income rises to $22,400 for women who earned bachelors degrees and averages $30,200 for women with master's degrees (U.S. Bureau of the Census 1994).

Today more women than men are enrolled in U.S. colleges and universities and the proportion of professional degrees earned by women has increased sharply (U.S. Bureau of the Census 1994). Such educational attainment varies by race and ethnicity. For example, in 1994, 25 percent of white women (age 25 and older) in the labor force had obtained a four-year college degree, compared with 17 and 13 percent, respectively, for African American and Latina women. A much larger share of white women (30 percent) than African American (21 percent) or Latina (17 percent) women held managerial and professional specialty jobs in 1994 (U.S. Department of Labor 1995a). While formal educational credentials are often crucial to obtaining high- paying management or professional positions, their role in assisting an entrepreneur in succeeding in business is less clear.

The women in this book have a relatively high degree of educational attainment. The percentages of white and Latina women vary across educational attainment categories (Table 4.7). More Latina than white women earned only a high school diploma, and a lower percentage of Latina than white women earned graduate degrees. We know that social connections and educational attainment impact one's position within the occupational structure, and that certain positions, such as professional, are inaccessible to those without advanced credentials. But how important is educational attainment to an entrepreneur? How significant is advanced education or training to achieving entrepreneurial success?

The 16 women who obtained the highest levels of education, master's and PhDs, tend to cluster in high technology, accounting and financial planning, and psychology and health care services. Of those women with advanced degrees, half (one Latina and seven white women) earned master's degrees in business administration (MBAs) and all own financially-related or high technology businesses.

Table 4.7 Educational Attainment of White and Latina Women in My Study, 1997.

Educational Attainment	White (N=67)	Latina (N=22)
Percentage Distribution		
High school diploma only	16.4	31.8
Some college	22.4	22.7
Bachelors degree	38.8	40.9
Graduate degree	22.4	4.5
Of graduate degree holders		
Master of arts	40.0	0.0
Master of science	6.7	0.0
Master of business admin	46.7	100.0*
PhD	6.7	0.0

*This individual also holds a master's degree in engineering.

Recall Claudia Sanchez, who established a manufacturing firm with her husband, Ricardo, in 1991. Claudia and Ricardo had the technical expertise to run their business, but lacked basic management and finance knowledge. "I thought, "Well, if I wanted to start a company, there are lots of things that one can do to start up." I needed more knowledge about management, accounting, and finance and marketing and things," Claudia explains. She enrolled in an MBA program that assisted her in developing a research and business plan. Claudia argues that without the knowledge and skills gained through the MBA program, their business would not have been able to take off and progress as smoothly as it has. The business plan Claudia created during her MBA program allowed her to target San Diego as the best business climate for their new venture.

There are several other women who have MBAs and do financial consulting or accounting. Unlike Claudia, these other women feel that the MBA offers little in the way of assisting them as entrepreneurs; rather, they point to other more significant keys to business ownership. First, some explain that remaining licensed or credentialed in their particular field is most crucial to their entrepreneurial success. Second, other women with advanced degrees emphasize staying current in business associations and networking with associates. Social capital is deemed more crucial by these women than knowledge gained from advanced education.

Barbara Klaus is the one woman in this study who holds a master's of science degree. After earning her master's degree, Barbara worked consecutively for two large companies, each for about 10 years. Three years ago Barbara, then age 40, bought a health services company that currently has over 65 employees and generates over $1 million annually in revenues. Similar to many women in this study who hold MBAs, Barbara feels that her master's degree hasn't helped her significantly as an entrepreneur. In fact, she describes her degree as totally invisible. Barbara explains further:

> I don't have a PhD, this would carry more clout. But I was at [TechMax] previously and from that company I developed a really good network. A network is so crucial. And you also have to have an understanding and practice total quality management. I hate to use textbook terms, but it's true. You have to do that, doing what the customer wants.

Barbara stresses the benefits of social capital, a really good network, above the credential of an advanced degree for business success. As Bourdieu argues, the yield of the educational qualification depends on the social capital that can be used to back it up.

Another woman in this study, Dina Berst, earned a master's degree in health education and is currently planning to return to school for her PhD. Like Barbara, she argues that a PhD carries more clout in the field of health: "What I really need as a sole proprietor is to be at the doctoral level."

The women (39 percent) who earned only bachelors degrees are in a wide array of industries. White women with bachelors degrees own businesses in real estate appraisal, financial and management consulting, accounting services, training and development, computer consulting, architecture and interior design, and exercise and fitness. The Latina women with bachelors degrees are found in catering, publishing, translation services, computer services, construction, and retail trade.

Like the women with advanced graduate degrees, the women with bachelors degrees spoke of the importance of professional licensing in certain industries. Doris Lamont owns a real estate appraisal business and recalls that "at one time, we didn't need formal training or a license. But now you have to have a certain amount of experience for certification and take courses worth 45 hours." Gail Mayfield and Jayne Kanter own architecture firms, another industry governed by licensing regulations. Gail has owned her own architecture firm since 1984, and makes it clear that without experience and a license, you don't have a business. Gail was able to turn to her parents, both independent architects, for additional help with the financial side of the business. Other women in financial advising and construction spoke of the licensing process in these areas too.

Over half the women with bachelors degrees underscore the significance of developing interpersonal and communication skills for entrepreneurial success. This is especially true for Margot James, who has owned a management consulting business since 1987.

> You need to take a well-rounded, renaissance approach to business. . . . What's
> key to me is the ability to communicate orally and in writing. You have to be
> able to create as well as make presentations. It's not so much about a degree
> than work experience that allows you to develop these skills.

Margot mentions that the college degree is not as significant as work experience in gaining communication skills. But we should keep in mind that, more often than not, you need a college degree to gain this kind of work experience to begin with or even be interviewed for such a position.

Sheila Murray agrees that communication skills gained from work experience are most important to a successful entrepreneur. A number of years after earning her bachelors degree in business, Sheila opened her management consulting business in 1994.

> Experience is undervalued. Often times formal credentials are overvalued. I
> have a business degree with an emphasis in marketing that gives me credibility,
> and allows me to get my foot in the door.

Sheila makes an important point about educational credentials expressed by many other women entrepreneurs. Educational credentials offer the business owner credibility in the eyes of clients, customers, or associates. As Bourdieu argues, obtaining educational credentials offers these women an important kind of cultural benefit: prestige or distinction. Yet, according to these women, the actual knowledge gained from these educational experiences offers the entrepreneur little comparable benefit.

There are many women entrepreneurs who had earned bachelors degrees, yet still lacked business skills. A handful of these women, including Rachel Maxwell, sought help from local business development associations. While Rachel had years of training in fitness, she describes herself as being somewhere between kindergarten and fourth grade in terms of business knowledge. Taking workshops and seminars from local business development groups allowed Rachel to develop a business plan and learn how to recruit customers. This knowledge allowed her to open a successful exercise business which grosses between $50,000 and $100,000 annually.

A good number of women (43 percent) did not have a college degree. Some of these women viewed barriers to occupational advancement due to their lack of advanced educational credentials. For Aida Sandoval and Diane Mason, both with high school diplomas only, pretending to have college degrees opened up doors that led them to entrepreneurship in sales.

Forty-five-year-old Aida, a Latina who grew up just north of the U.S.-Mexico border, was never encouraged to earn a college degree when she was younger. In fact, her family discouraged her from attending college.

> All of my social upbringing. . . . All my girlfriends were in the same position I was, they didn't go away to college. My mother thought the idea of dorms was horrible. . . . I got married and moved to San Diego. We had our first child and I was a stay-at-home mom. I got pregnant again. I had our son. A year and a half later, I had this thing about getting out. My husband was successful and coming home with all these stories and I felt out of it.

After seven years of marriage, Aida and her husband divorced and Aida was faced with entering the work force with two children under age 5. She took a secretarial position that left her feeling bored and antsy.

> What is the only way to make a lot of money and not have a degree? Sales. I wanted to work for a company. . . . In order to get an interview, I lied about my education. They wouldn't interview you without a college degree. They didn't check and I felt confident that I was qualified. They hired me and I was very successful and I did that for about five years.

By initially lying about her educational qualifications, Aida gained an interview that led to a sales position and the experience necessary to eventually branch out on her own. Since 1987, Aida has owned her own sales company that she started in her home to have more flexibility with her children. "It seems like to get a job in sales you need a college degree," Aida argues, "but I felt confident enough that I was qualified. You have to know how to sell."

Likewise, Diane Mason, a 39-year-old white woman, lied about her educational qualifications in order to obtain her first sales position. Diane was married shortly after graduating from high school. She explains, "I became a waitress full-time for four years to support my husband and make his dreams happen." Diane then spent a couple of years as a sales associate. "Being in sales is so bottom-line oriented, anyone who brings in money will be okay." But Diane points out that she lied about having a college degree in order to get her first sales job. Using the skills she has learned in sales, Diane has owned a consulting company for the past three years. For Diane and Aida, the most important skill for them as entrepreneurs is the ability to sell, a skill they feel one can master without a college degree. These sentiments are echoed by four other women who are in sales, but have earned bachelors degrees. One expresses, "You don't need to have a degree, but you do need to know how to sell."

Aida and Diane, both high school graduates, argue that even though many sales jobs require a college degree for an interview, the most crucial skill is the ability to sell. Likewise, the highest level of education that Celia Robles achieved was a high school degree. Celia, who owns a business in which she sells her services as a violinist, explains that talent is the most important credential in the music industry. Thirty-two-year-old Patricia Stevens, who owns a photography business with her husband agrees, "You need to have a kind of artistic knowledge of what you're doing." Other industries of women in this book who earned only high school diplomas include: beauty and massage services, domestic cleaning, and catering and floral businesses.

Obviously, some industries are closed to entrepreneurs without advanced educational degrees. For example, without a college degree, you can't open your own architectural firm or psychotherapy practice. But many more fields don't have professional gatekeeping. The women in these fields view an advanced degree as a way primarily to gain greater credibility. Many women with degrees do not apply the knowledge they learned in school to their businesses. And many women point out that attaining educational credentials is but one way to gain credibility as an entrepreneur. Most women, with and without degrees, view the social networking and communication skills gained through work experience as most crucial to gaining credibility, respect, and distinction as an entrepreneur.

EDUCATION AND GROSS BUSINESS RECEIPTS

We know that higher levels of educational attainment translate into higher average incomes for workers in the United States. Is there any relationship between level of educational attainment of an entrepreneur and overall business sales and receipts?

Table 4.8 Educational Attainment of Women in My Study and Gross Receipts, 1997.

Gross Receipts	Educational Attainment				
	High school Diploma Only	Some College	Bachelors Degree	Graduate Degree	Row Total
Percentage Distribution					
Less than $25,000	16. 7	20. 0	0. 0	12. 5	10. 2
$25,000 - $100,000	61. 1	50. 0	64. 7	50. 0	58. 0
$100,000 - $500,000	16. 7	20. 0	20. 6	25. 0	20. 5
More than $500,000	5. 6	10. 0	14. 7	12. 5	11. 4
	100. 0	100. 0	100. 0	100. 0	100. 0

Most businesses in this study (58 percent) gross between $25,000 and $100,000 in sales and receipts annually (Table 4.8). The highest proportion of

women in each educational attainment level fall into this receipt category. About
11 percent of women's businesses gross over $500,000. Interestingly, a higher
proportion of women with college degrees than without are in this receipt
category (15 percent of bachelors and 13 percent of graduate degree recipients
compared to 6 percent of women with high school diplomas only and 10 percent
of women with some college).

There doesn't appear to be a clear cut pattern between educational
attainment and business receipts, mainly because this relationship is complicated
by the industry in which an entrepreneur does business. Of those with bachelors
degrees, 36 percent have businesses that gross more than $100,000. For women
without bachelors degrees, 26 percent gross more than $100,000 (chi-square test
is not statistically significant; Fisher's exact test: $p=0.36$; Phi coefficient=.10).

There are some high-receipt industries which require little formal education
and no licensing. Take Jennifer Miller's flower shop, for example. Thirty-six-
year-old Jennifer earned her high school diploma and went to work as a floral
designer right out of high school. She never felt the pull of college, and after
taking some time off to raise her children, Jennifer opened her flower shop over
a year ago. Her gross business sales and receipts are higher than many other
women: They range from $200,000 to $500,000 annually. Gross sales and
receipts (rather than net) are used most frequently to measure the financial
success of small businesses. By the nature of its business, flower shops like
Jennifer's tend to have high gross sales and receipts. Jennifer explains what it
takes to run a successful flower shop:

> You need to be artistic. You need to understand that what you put into an
> arrangement, it all adds up. You could give your shirt away if you're not
> careful. A lot of people don't realize that the little things you add to an
> arrangement, the moss, the iddy biddy things, they take extra pennies and
> dimes, and soon your money is down the drain. You have to know how to price
> things and how to buy too. You have high gross profits, but a lower percentage
> of profit.

Businesses like Jennifer's don't require their owners to have high levels of
education. Yet, by the nature of their business, they have relatively high gross
sales and receipts. While perhaps the exception, Jennifer Miller still makes an
interesting case. What would a college degree offer Jennifer as an entrepreneur?
Would the credibility or distinction it brings really make her a more successful
entrepreneur? Most of the women entrepreneurs in this book would answer "No"
to this question.

GENDERED BIASES OF BUSINESS

I have discussed the role that educational attainment plays in the experiences of women entrepreneurs, but how significant is embodied cultural capital in the form of dispositions, mannerisms, and tastes? Bourdieu (1986) argues that the accumulation of cultural capital in the embodied state "presupposes a process of em-bodiment, incorporation which insofar as it implies a labor of inculcation and assimilation, costs time, time which must be invested personally by the investor" (p. 244). Bourdieu (1986) emphasizes that to acquire embodied cultural capital one must "work on oneself...Like the acquisition of a muscular physique or a suntan, it cannot be done secondhand" (p. 244). What is the nature of the embodied capital needed to succeed in business?

We know that historically business ownership has been a male domain; in the early part of the century, businesses were often owned and managed by men. In the case of family-run businesses, women frequently worked as unpaid workers or silent partners. As more women entered the workforce throughout this century, we have seen obvious and radical shifts in women's work patterns. Today, about 60 percent of women (age 16 and older) in the United States participate in paid work, compared to 75 percent of men (Dunn 1997). Although women continue to be employed in a far more narrow range of low-pay occupations than men, they still have made gains in management, professional jobs, and male-dominated, blue-collar occupations.

Women in such nontraditional occupations often encounter male-oriented work cultures that assume female inferiority (Pierce 1995; Rosenberg et al 1993; Swan 1994; Swerdlow 1989; Wright 1996). Jennifer Pierce's (1995) study of lawyers finds that litigation rests on masculinizing practices such as aggression and intimidation, and that women lawyers are often viewed as less capable because the job requires these masculinized, highly-prized forms of labor practices. Elaine Swan (1994) argues that because the dominant model of management is still associated with the masculine-identified attributes of aggression, assertiveness, and competition, women managers are disadvantaged because they represent a highly visible "Other" or "matter out of place." Likewise, Marian Swerdlow's (1989) study of rapid transit operators, a traditionally male-dominated, blue-collar job, illustrates how women's presence generates tensions for men by threatening assumptions of male supremacy. In these work environments, often times dispositions or attributes associated with "female" are degraded and disparaged.[4]

Similar to women waged or salaried employees, women entrepreneurs encounter diverse work environments depending upon the industry in which they own their business. Research on women entrepreneurs finds that women who establish businesses in nontraditional industries, such as construction or finance, must often struggle to overcome the belief that women are not as serious as men about business (Hisrich and O'Brien 1981). How might women entrepreneurs in nontraditional industries maximize the embodied cultural capital of dispositions and mannerisms and use such capital to their benefit in business?

I identified 25 women (19 white and six Latina) who describe themselves as operating businesses in male-dominated industries, in which they feel like one of the relatively few women entrepreneurs. These industries include: construction, manufacturing, financial and computer services, art and architecture, and high technology. All of these women had stories of sexism and discrimination to tell, which is unfortunately nothing new. We know that on-the-job discrimination and other forms of sexist experiences tend to be higher among women who are structurally isolated or in token positions (Rosenberg et al 1993).

All of the women in these industries emphasize the importance of a friendly disposition, being kind and good-natured, in order to win over male peers, colleagues, and clients. Far from being confrontational or adversarial, these women respond to sexist male-oriented cultures by "killing them with kindness" as opposed to lashing back with aggression or defensive comments.

Cynthia Valdes started a construction business with her husband in 1983.

> I get people who assume I don't know anything about the job. I have been teased by high profile contractors. I'm the butt of the cute, little jokes. I take it good-naturedly. There's really no point in retaliating. Hopefully you make your mark through your work. But it's still a very macho industry. You learn to weed out the people who don't respect you.

Cynthia emphasizes the importance of having a personable disposition when dealing with contractors or customers.

Jayne Kanter, owner of an architecture firm since 1992, has an approach similar to Cynthia's. Jayne feels that it is best to respond to sexist behavior by letting the men know what is acceptable or unacceptable behavior without acting like "an emotional, hysterical woman."

> On the job site, there's still whistling. It's 1997 and they are still whistling. But I don't mind that much, as long as they don't say something rude. . . . But sometimes they [contractors] have a hard time taking you seriously. They don't cuss in front of you, they put on the gentleman act, and if they say something you take offense to and you get mad, they'll get really mad back. You can't be an emotional, hysterical woman and get attention. If you start this, "He hurt my feelings," and all that bitchy stuff, it doesn't work with them. They see you as a woman and you are now viewed as below zero.

Cynthia and Jayne do not advocate allowing sexist behavior to occur unchecked. But they contend that responding to such behavior in a firm, yet good-natured way is the best approach to maximizing one's respect and credibility.

Doris Lamont also finds this to be the case. Doris owns a home-based real estate appraisal business with her husband. Doris explains that sometimes people are surprised that she, being a woman, owns part of a business in such a male-dominated field.

> There are times when people treat you differently. When Hal and I will enter a home and they'll think that I'm the assistant and Hal's the appraiser. There are still those stereotypes out there. Usually I don't want to offend the person. I'll just laugh. And Hal will joke, "No, I'm assisting her." People will always have their biases. You have to be smart and savvy and work things to your benefit.

For Doris, working things to your benefit doesn't necessarily mean directly confronting sexist behavior or attitudes. Rather, she and Hal attempt to turn such situations around by making jokes that place him in the expected female assistant role. Doris argues that sometimes in these situations she will also "do the softer side," meaning talk in a more subdued way in order to get people comfortable with her.

Claudia Sanchez owns a manufacturing business with her husband. Like Doris, Claudia also finds that people often mistake her for an assistant or secretary. They often act surprised when they find out that she is the owner. Claudia explains, "You have to get past that because you just don't have time to sit down and lecture everybody." Similar to Doris, Claudia mostly shrugs these attitudes off.

Gwen Means, who owns a pension firm, echoes similar sentiments.

> There are still some attitudes out there. You have to figure out which fights you're going to fight. If I spent all my time dealing with the attitudes and fighting all the fights, I wouldn't be running a business, I'd be changing the world. My attitude is, I'll go around you. Go around the attitudes and go to someone else.

This ability of controlling who you work with, going around the attitudes and going to someone else, was underscored by all the women in male-dominated industries. Gwen continues, "I have fired clients. I'll say our professional way of doing things doesn't mix. I like the empowerment of being an owner."

Vicki Torres further details the importance of a friendly, good-natured disposition in business. When Vicki bought into an electrical business, she recognized the possible negative ramifications of a woman-owned electrical company in such a male-dominated industry. In fact, when Vicki first bought the business and became the new business partner of Dan Braverman, she didn't want many people to know about the change.

> When I first bought [the business] . . . I didn't dare tell a soul. I mean my partner, my supervisors knew, but I didn't want to tell the employees. I didn't want them to be any different and I didn't want to be any different. I'd rather them think that Dan owns the business just like it was before and there's no change.

Vicki wanted the business to appear stable and felt that her partnership with Dan might jeopardize that appearance. Over several months, employees and other industry contacts were told of the ownership change. Vicki now sees the advantages of having a male-female partnership in the electrical industry. She feels that the most important attributes she brings to the business are her communication skills and her open and friendly approach with people.

> My partner is not a communicative person and so, when the business was growing, we were having to market ourselves and we were having to be nice to people that came in the front door and it's like, now we have to smile. We never had to do that before. That's something, I've always liked people, I've always enjoyed getting out and meeting and talking. There for a while, last year, I was out cold calling [people who didn't know the company]. I was making cold calls and I loved it.

Vicki finds that at some industry conventions, she'll be one of few women. In these situations her strategy is to "walk into a room and just start talking to everybody. I just do it, and it kind of bugs my competitors. But you know for the most part, I'll walk up to them and shake hands and say, 'Hi Jim. How you doing? Been busy?'"

A number of other women share this approach. Displaying friendliness to adversaries or competitors appears to be one strategy for success among women entrepreneurs in nontraditional industries. Even though some of her competitors have been underhanded in getting business accounts she secured, Aida Sandoval responds to her competition by being very polite. Christine Myers, owner of a collection services business, handled an incident with a chauvinistic colleague in a similar way. Christine explains,"He never invited me in on conversations. I flatly reminded him that I was an officer in the organization." She emphasizes,

"I put it to him in a nice way. He now pats me on the back. We became friends." Art gallery owner Cindy Kelley also finds that, although some people in the art world don't take women as seriously, it's best to be "nice and polite" if you want to sell yourself and your work. According to Cindy, the art world is still very much a man's domain.

Cindy also underscores the importance of establishing a close rapport with her clients. "I try to get to know them. I think I have tended to become friends over time with a lot of clients." Shelley Johnson, owner of a consulting company since 1995, agrees that it is important to open up to clients. "I like to let people know that I'm human. I'll share a story about the family. Some prefer to dwell on that, some don't. You have to read your customers, pay attention to their needs," Shelley explains.

All of the women who have businesses in nontraditional industries emphasize the significance of a friendly, good-natured disposition and polite mannerisms. These dispositions and mannerisms appear to be key cultural capital for women entrepreneurs in securing respect in such nontraditional industries. Even though they encounter sexist attitudes and behaviors, these women agree that you need to maintain a positive, professional demeanor to succeed as a woman entrepreneur in these industries. For these women, this means sometimes developing strategies for dealing with sexist comments or behavior. It also appears to be the case that having a male business partner may be a way for women entrepreneurs to gain a foothold in nontraditional industries.

In their study of women lawyers, Rosenberg et al. (1993) contend that for years women in male-dominated occupations have been told to be patient, take on the values of men in their positions, or downplay their feminist identities. They argue that women who do this, who "play the careerist game, may unintentionally reinforce those aspects of organizational and professional culture that encourage men to believe they can control women or drive them out through discrimination and manipulation" (Rosenberg et al. 1993:431). To a certain extent, the women in male-dominated industries in this book play the careerist game by overlooking or downplaying some sexually offensive circumstances. Yet, as entrepreneurs, these women also have and use the power to choose between clients or associates. They often purposefully avoid doing business with those men who display such behavior.

CONCLUSION

This chapter offers analysis of the economic, social, and cultural capital used by white and Latina women entrepreneurs. Overwhelmingly these entrepreneurial women are from middle class families and have been able to tap into combinations of economic, social, and cultural capital necessary to become an entrepreneur.

First, economic capital refers to resources that are directly convertible into money and that may be institutionalized in the form of property rights (Bourdieu 1986). Most women used personal savings or credit as their primary financial source when starting their businesses. A higher percentage of white than Latina women used personal resources. Over half of the women began their businesses in their homes, which cut down on start-up costs. About 11 percent relied on the economic contribution of parents or siblings for business start-up capital. As children, these women tended to be involved in productive activities that contributed in some way to the family income. A slightly higher percentage of Latina than white women used family sources. Very few women turned to formal lending institutions for start-up capital.

This study also analyzes social capital, valuable resources in the form of social connections or networks of acquaintance, mutual trust, and recognition. My assessment of social capital includes examination of women entrepreneurs' mentors. Those women who relied on mentors most often found mentors in the same industry. Women entrepreneurs primarily rely on mentors who are men or a combination of both men and women mentors. Less than one-fourth of the women with mentors named only other women as sources of mentorship. While many women turned to all-women business organizations for networking, most found that these lacked concrete advice and assistance for running a business. Latina women were more likely to own a business in which their husbands participate than the white women. Women with dependent children at home were less likely to have business partnerships with their husbands.

This study also offers a starting point for thinking about the complexities of cultural capital in the lives of women entrepreneurs. With respect to institutionalized cultural capital, women view a college or graduate degree as a way to gain greater credibility, but many point out that attaining educational credentials is but one way to gain such respect. Most women view networking and communication skills gained through work experience as most crucial to gaining distinction as an entrepreneur. To assess the embodied cultural capital of dispositions, mannerisms, and tastes for women entrepreneurs' experiences, I specifically examine how women entrepreneurs in male-dominated industries use such capital to their advantage. I find that women in these industries emphasize the importance of friendliness, kindness, and being good-natured in order to win over male colleagues and clients. These women respond to sexist male-oriented cultures by continuing to display a positive attitude, joking about inappropriate sexist attitudes, or using their business owner status to limit contact with offensive clients or associates.

CHAPTER 5

Patterns of Latina Entrepreneurship

Many studies on entrepreneurs look at women's compared to men's entrepreneurship, with little attention to racial or ethnic variations (Aldrich et al 1995), or examine entrepreneurship among one particular ethnic or immigrant group (Light and Bonacich 1988; Mar 1991; Park 1997). Throughout this study, I have focused on both white and Latina women entrepreneurs, examining similarities and differences in their pathways to entrepreneurship and use of various forms of capital. This comparative focus is crucial to understanding how entrepreneurship might differ between ethnic groups.

This study also provides a unique opportunity to look more closely at Latina entrepreneurship in the formal economy. This has been the topic of little study. In their overview of Chicanas/os in the U.S. economy since 1970, Rochin and de la Torre (1996) argue that although the journal *Hispanic Businesses* has tracked the economic successes of Latinos in a variety of businesses, we still know relatively little about Latino entrepreneurs and enterprises.

There has been considerable research on Latina immigrant women and their economic ventures in the informal U.S. economy (Hondagneu-Sotelo 1994; Romero 1992; Ruiz 1987). There also have been studies addressing Latina homeworkers, women employed at home by large companies, such as those in garment manufacturing (Fernandez-Kelley and Garcia 1989). This chapter, devoted entirely to the Latina women in the study, furthers our knowledge of Latina women in the U.S. work force by allowing us to understand more fully the dynamics behind their patterns of entrepreneurship in the formal economy.

LATINAS IN THE U.S. LABOR MARKET

Latinos are the fastest growing ethnic group in the United States, and will likely outnumber African Americans by the year 2010 (Romero 1997). A look at Latina women in the United States reveals that their labor force participation rate has increased over recent years. Although labor force participation of Latina

97

women (over age 16) increased from 47 percent in 1983 to 52 percent in 1993, these rates are still about six percentage points lower than those of other women (U.S. Bureau of the Census 1993a). The increase in their participation over time has been attributed to economic need, increased employment opportunities, and the erosion of cultural patterns emphasizing women's traditional roles in the family (Ortiz 1994; Zavella 1987).

Ethnic differences in women's labor force participation also have been linked to differences in educational attainment (Ortiz and Santana-Cooney 1984). The most educated groups of women are those with the highest levels of labor force activity. For instance, 85 percent of all women with four-year degrees were in the labor force in 1994 (Herz and Wootton 1996). While Latinas' educational attainment levels are lower than those of white women, there has been some increase in higher education for Latinas. In 1991, among high school graduates, 39 percent of Hispanic women ages 18 to 24 enrolled in college, up nearly 10 percent from 1990 (Carter and Wilson 1993). During that same period, the rate for associates and bachelors degrees conferred increased 5 percent and 12 percent respectively for Hispanic women (Carter and Wilson 1993).

Similar to other groups of women in the U.S. labor market, Latina women are more likely to be in technical, sales, and administrative support occupations than in any other occupational category (U.S. Bureau of the Census 1993b). Latinas are more likely to be in service occupations compared to white women (24 percent and 15 percent, respectively) and less likely to be in better-paying managerial and professional occupations (17 percent and 30 percent, respectively) (U.S. Bureau of the Census 1993b). Latinas are overrepresented in low-paying jobs susceptible to seasonal fluctuations, like domestic work and garment factory work (Segura 1994). The median weekly earnings of Latinas was about $100 less than that of non-Latinas in 1992: $299 for Latinas versus $393 for non-Latinas (Rochin and de la Torre 1996).

Closer examination of the Latina population reveals the significant impact of citizenship and immigration status on work-related characteristics. A recent survey of 803 Latinas and 422 Anglo women in Orange County, California, found that Latina immigrants were younger than Latina citizens and Anglo women, had less years of education, and were more likely to be in the reproductive stages of the life cycle (Chavez et al 1997). Undocumented Latinas were more likely than other Latinas and Anglo women to be unemployed and looking for work (Chavez et al 1997). Less than a quarter of the undocumented

Table 5.1. Occupations of Women, Hispanic Origin and White (Not of Hispanic Origin), 1990

Occupation	Hispanic Origin	White (Not of Hispanic Origin)
Total employed (thousands)	3 669	41 499
Percentage Distribution		
Managerial, Professional	**17.0**	**29.8**
Executive, Administrative, Managerial	7.6	12.1
Professional Specialty	9.4	17.6
Technical, Sales, Administrative Support	**39.1**	**44.9**
Technicians and Related Support	2.7	3.7
Sales Occupations	11.4	13.0
Administrative Support	25.1	28.2
Service Occupations	**23.5**	**15.1**
Private Household	3.1	.6
Protective Service	.5	.5
Other Service	19.9	14.0
Precision Production, Craft, Repair	**3.5**	**2.1**
Operators, Fabricators, Laborers	**15.2**	**7.3**
Machine Operators, Assemblers, Inspectors	11.6	4.8
Transportation, Material Moving	.7	.9
Handlers, Equipment Cleaners, Helpers Laborers	2.9	1.6
Farming, Fishing, Forestry	**1.6**	**.9**

Source: U.S. Bureau of the Census, 1993b.

immigrants were employed full-time (Chavez et al 1997). While the majority of documented and undocumented Latina immigrants worked in private household and other services without job-related benefits, the most common occupation among Latina citizens and Anglo women was clerical work (Chavez et al 1997). Most (76 percent) of the undocumented Latinas earned under $15,000 annually and less than one percent earned more than $35,000 annually, the income level above which the majority of Latina citizens and Anglo women clustered (Chavez et al 1997).

The question of why Latinas and women of other ethnic backgrounds are occupationally segregated is the subject of some debate. The human capital explanation argues that job mobility and wages are the result of individual characteristics, such as education, training, years of work experience, interests, and attitudes. Human capital theorists assert that women choose jobs that are less demanding because they expect the need for flexibility due to child rearing and other domestic responsibilities (Becker 1985; Mincer and Polachek 1978). This perspective fails to acknowledge that workers do not have equal opportunity to acquire human capital and do not have the same access to job information (Segura 1994). Denise Segura (1986) argues that Latinas in the labor force experience triple oppression defined as "the interplay among class, race, and gender, whose cumulative effects place women of color in a subordinate social and economic position relative to men of color and the majority white population" (p. 48). Because of their minority status, Latina women may be more likely to serve as a disadvantaged labor pool in positions in which personnel turnover and job instability are high and wages and job advancement are low.

Focusing specifically on Chicanas and Mexican immigrant women in the United States, Denise Segura (1994) argues that the labor market structure limits these women's employment and job mobility opportunities. In her study of 40 Latina women, Segura (1994) critiques human capital's emphasis on individual rational choice by arguing that Latina women's occupational segregation is often reinforced by a channeling process that includes: schooling that promotes women's place in the home; training programs that prompt women to enter jobs primarily occupied by women; and family dynamics, such as husband's dislike of wives working with men. Segura (1994) argues that "schooling did not impart a sense of employment options outside those traditionally ascribed to women. . . . Family dynamics also upheld women's participation in female-dominated jobs" (p. 107). This intersection of macro and micro social dynamics posed significant barriers to Latina women's job attachment and advancement (Segura 1994). Portes and Truelove (1987) further argue for the significance of social relations and networks in accounting for occupational patterns: family and friends may direct new entrants into jobs similar to their own.

Were the Latina women entrepreneurs in this book subject to a similar channeling process? There is a noticeable difference in terms of education and work patterns between different generations of these women. Sixteen of the 22 Latina women can be characterized as "women of the sixties," a term Katherine Newman uses to describe women who were born after World War II and into the early 1950s. Many middle class Americans who grew up during this time spent their childhood years in homes relatively free of economic hardship, especially compared to their parents who grew up in the Depression (Newman 1988, 1993). Five Latina women in this study can be characterized as members of "the Reagan generation," those who entered adolescence and young adulthood during the 1980s when Ronald Reagan was President of the United States (Newman 1993).

Similar career and family paths exist among the 16 Latinas who came of age in the 1960s. The channeling process that Segura describes begins at a young age.

Table 5.2 Selected Characteristics by Generation for the Latinas in My Study, 1997.

	Sixties Generation (N=16)	Reagan Generation (N=5)	Total (N =21)
Mean Age (years)	49	32	
Percentage Distribution			
Born Outside the United States	18. 8	40. 0	23. 8 (5)
Mexico	66. 7	100. 0	
Japan	33. 3		
Educational Attainment			
High School/Some College	56. 3	40. 0	52. 4 (11)
Bachelors/Graduate Degree	43. 7	60. 0	47. 6 (10)
Marital Status			
Never Married	18. 8	40. 0	23. 8 (5)
Married	68. 8	60. 0	66. 7 (14)
Divorced	12. 5		9. 5 (2)
Children (Currently)			
None	18. 8	60. 0	28. 6 (6)
Children < Age 18	12. 5	40. 0	19. 0 (4)
Children > Age 18	68. 8		52. 4 (11)

Note: One Latina is not represented in the table. I characterize one Latina, age 70, as postwar generation. Her highest level of educational attainment is a high school diploma. She is married with children over age 18.

Like other women of the sixties generation, many of these Latinas spoke of never being encouraged to pursue college degrees or to seek professional or managerial jobs when they were growing up. Vicki Torres recalls that the expectation was for women to get married and have children. "My thinking in high school was that I would not work when I married," Vicki states.

Despite the lack of encouragement to pursue advanced education when they were younger, seven of these 16 Latinas eventually earned bachelors degrees, three have taken some college courses, and six have high school diplomas only. Most of the sixties generation women were married in their twenties and worked in clerical positions until the birth of their first child, at which time they stopped working for several years.

Eva Cruz's experiences typify these patterns. Eva, now age 54, recalls her parents' hopes for her future while growing up in Mexico.

> I came here [to San Diego] when I was 15 for school and then I went back. . . . In Mexico a lot of kids come here. I graduated from a Catholic school here and then went back. My Dad wanted us to learn English. It was assumed that I would grow up, that I would get married and have children. That's the way it used to be in Mexico. But my father thought that women should have skills too. He felt that women should have skills to go to work. He never meant for us to have a college education, just basic skills, and we [me and my sisters] all had secretarial skills. My brother, he went to college and is now a surgeon.

In Eva's family, gender was clearly a factor in determining which children went to college. The family used a number of resources to send the children to high school in the United States. But these resources were not used for advanced education in the case of the daughters. Eva followed a path like that of her mother. She married young and used her secretarial skills for extra family income. Eva married at age 20 and moved to the U.S. with her husband, who planned to earn a university degree. Eva then applied her secretarial skills by working full-time in a number of offices. Eva explains that she has always worked full-time through her marriage, except for the first few years when her children were young.

After years of working as a secretary, Eva became disillusioned with her advancement potential. "I saw the type of people hired for administrative jobs, and I was more qualified than they were," Eva explains. But, according to her boss, she couldn't be promoted without a college degree.

> So I was talking about it for a while, going back to school. I was talking with my friends about it and one said, "What do you want? To be 50 years old and a secretary or 50 years old and an attorney?" My husband said, "I don't think you should be telling everybody that you are going back to school, because you're never going."

Despite her husband's lack of encouragement, Eva enrolled in business courses at a local college. Ironically, it was Eva's mother who offered her the most encouragement at this time and gave her the money for college tuition. "By this time I was in my 30s and the whole family was so proud of me because I was the first female to get a degree." Once she graduated with a business degree, Eva was promoted to manager and remained in management positions until she opened her party planning business in 1991.

Like Eva, Aida Sandoval, now age 45, explains that when growing up, she was never encouraged to go to college, although her brothers were. Aida was born in the United States and grew up in a small town just north of the Mexican border. Aida had a stay-at-home mom and her dad was an accountant. Aida explains, "I wanted to get married, wanted to leave. I was always chaperoned and brought up in a very strict home. . . . I married an American . . . not a Mexican. It was okay because he was related to a well-known family." After Aida got married, she and her husband moved to San Diego where he took business courses at a local university, and she found a secretarial job to help pay for household expenses. "My ultimate goal was not to work, but to stay at home and be a mom. . . . We had our first child and I was a stay-at-home mom. I got pregnant again."

After seven years of marriage, Aida and her husband divorced, and Aida was faced with entering the work force with two young children. She went back to clerical work, but soon found this repetitive and unrewarding. Unlike Eva who returned to school, Aida never made it to college. In fact, she lied about her educational attainment, saying that she did earn a college degree, in order to get a promotion into sales. Wanting to be more available to her young children, Aida decided to establish a home-based business. She relied on several industry contacts and customers for initial work. "Some clients followed me when I went out on my own," Aida explains.

Gloria Morales, age 42, was born in the United States and grew up in a family that encouraged her to pursue a career in elementary school teaching. Teaching, like nursing and social work, have been the more traditionally accepted semi-professions for women (Dunn 1997). Compared to professionals, such as lawyers and doctors, these semi-professions are lower in the occupational hierarchy and lack the power and rewards necessary to gain recognition as full professions (Dunn 1997).

Gloria started to take education courses in college when she met and married her husband. Soon after, they had a son and then separated. Gloria never finished her degree.

> My husband and I separated, and I had an 8 month old son. So there was no way I could handle both. My own support network fell apart at that point because my child care was predicated on both in-laws and my parents being able to take care of my son. . . . From that point, I felt I had to primarily raise my son. And I was determined not to leave him for the next four years. So I stayed with my parents and raised my son and went back to work part time.

The most flexible kind of work Gloria could find involved secretarial and receptionist positions. Once her son was in elementary school, Gloria expanded her work hours to full time. In 1994, after working in clerical positions in human resources for most of her life, Gloria opened a personnel agency.

Like Gloria, 13 of these 16 women have children and all expressed deep concern for a mother's active participation in raising her children. Loretta Paredes was born in the United States and is currently married with three children who are over age 20. Loretta earned her bachelors degree in business before having a family. After having children, she devoted her full attention to raising them. "I waited until they were all in college before working at this [my own business]. My family always came first," states Loretta. "I wanted to be there for my children. They all turned out great. They never got into drugs and all went to college." Loretta attributes her children's success, in part, to her decision to stay at home while they were younger.

Two of these women still have young children at home and value the flexibility that comes with business ownership. Such is the case with Cynthia Valdes. Cynthia's father was in the military service and her mother was a homemaker. Born in Japan, Cynthia, age 45, grew up in the United States. When Cynthia's mother started to do clerical work for extra income, Cynthia recalls being cared for by her "traditional Hispanic" grandmother. Cynthia got married and started a home-based business in 1983 in order to stay at home and have flexibility with a family. "I always wanted to be home for the children," states Cynthia who has three children under age 11. "That's what's so good about being a business owner at home."

Unlike the Latina women of the sixties generation, the five Latinas who represent the Reagan Generation felt more encouragement to pursue advanced education when they were growing up. Two of the Reagan Generation women have bachelors degrees, two have taken some college courses, and one has a graduate degree. Three of these five women are married; two have young children.

Anita Jordan, now age 29, was born in Mexico. Anita moved to the U.S. when she was 8 years old with her mom, who was a homemaker, and her father, who was a businessman. Anita, her brothers, and her sister were all encouraged to go to college after high school. After earning an associates degree at a local community college, Anita married her husband and went to work as a real estate secretary. Anita explains that her dad made her transition from hourly-waged secretarial worker to business owner possible. "My dad knew I wanted to quit the other job, so he offered me a job at his bookstore, and then he offered it to us to buy," Anita explains. Anita now manages the bookstore, which she and her husband have owned since 1990. Anita and her husband have one school-age child, but pay for live-in child care help in order to balance work and family responsibilities.

Anita's father has been a constant source of financial and emotional support for her. Anita elaborates, "I get the most assistance from my dad. He has been in business all his life. He's the one I turn to when I have to make major decisions, like when we were moving to our new location. He gives me advice and then I make my own decisions." This kind of business-related relationship with a father is completely absent from the lives of the Latina women of the sixties generation. Their fathers and mothers encouraged them to assume domestic roles and learn basic clerical skills in the event that the household needed additional income.

Like Anita, Nora Ortiz, age 32, also was encouraged by her parents to pursue advanced education after high school. Both of her parents are Mexican American. Born in the United States, Nora grew up in New York and describes attending college as something that was expected of her.

> It was very expected in my family. It was understood. It was so ingrained enough it didn't even feel like a choice, and I am not saying that in a negative way. I knew that my way would be paved and that this would be made possible for me. I totally accepted that, my family are great believers in education.

Nora explains that her mother did not have an education beyond high school, and her father, who has a degree in biology, comes from a family of agricultural workers in California. "His family worked very hard in agriculture to provide for their children," explains Nora. Nora's father spent much of his career as a biologist and her mother was a homemaker when Nora was growing up. Once Nora and her sister were in high school, their mother took on some clerical jobs to increase the family income.

Nora argues that her parents felt that education would be the means to a better life.

> From my father's perspective, education would be the main frame in which I wouldn't have to do that difficult type of manual labor to support myself. So, my father has a college education and his parents worked very hard to put him through school. They wanted me to be sure I had the opportunity to go right out of high school onto college, and I was always told that they would do whatever it took to get me through.

The belief that education is significant to opening doors and creating opportunities is ingrained in the minds of many Americans. While educational opportunities are grossly unequal in this country, with public urban schools often receiving a fraction of the funding of wealthier suburban districts, Americans still view education as the great mechanism of equality and mobility (Kozol

1991). In the case of Nora's family, however, this rings true. Her father's family has a history in manual work, and after obtaining a bachelors degree, her father entered a relatively high-paying position. Nora's father's salary allowed her to live in a middle-class neighborhood with well-funded public elementary and secondary schools. She grew up knowing that money was being saved for her college tuition. Nora's bachelors degree in liberal studies led to several assistant-level public relations positions that allowed her to develop the skills and contacts necessary to open a public relations firm in 1996. Nora is married, but has no plans for children in the immediate future.

Thirty-three-year-old Marie Lopez explains that her family also wanted her to be well educated and self sufficient as she got older. Marie was born in San Diego, and still lives in the same neighborhood in which she grew up.

> My parents have always encouraged me to do just whatever I was happy at. My mom died . . . [but] even before, they both were very, they pushed me to go to school, finish college. In the Latino community, family is very important. The tradition is you get married, have kids, and stay home and raise the kids. My parents never did that. They always encouraged me to buy your own car, go out and travel, because you never know. I guess they just realized that the times are changing and you can't necessarily fall into that traditional role.

Marie describes the tradition for women to get married and stay home with their children. But, she also states that you can't necessarily fall into that traditional role because the times are changing. It is significant that both Marie and her brother were encouraged by their parents to go to college and expand their career opportunities. But, are younger Latina women being encouraged to pursue college degrees because ideologies about women's roles are changing? Or is it because the times are changing financially? In many families, women's incomes are needed to make ends meet. Both explanations have been put forth by sociologists to explain the rise of Latina women's participation in the work force. The gender role perspective argues that cultural norms, including machismo and familialism, have a major effect on Latina's labor force patterns and that increases in Latina's participation can be attributed to changing attitudes of gender roles (Mirande and Enrique 1979). More recent work underscores the importance of structural as well as cultural factors. This perspective argues that the gender role framework ignores that work and family relations are affected by structural changes. Many Latina women have a financial need to work and some live in female-headed households and provide the only household support despite traditional cultural norms to stay at home (Baca Zinn 1991; Zavella 1984).

The findings from my study suggest that both cultural and structural forces are crucial to women's work participation. Both generations of women were encouraged by their parents to learn skills that could be used in the labor market. But, for the older women of the sixties, gender ideologies dictated that women learn secretarial and clerical skills. The older women developed these basic skills at a young age so that, in times of crisis, they could go to work. The younger women also were encouraged by their parents to develop work-related skills. However, these women were prompted to earn advanced educational degrees and enter higher-paying positions. This reflects a significant change in beliefs about women's roles that mirrors a nationwide shift in gender ideology from the 1960s to the present.

INFORMAL AND HOME-BASED WORK

According to official statistics, increasing numbers of Latinas continue to enter the U.S. labor market. But, these figures do not accurately capture "under the table" positions commonly filled by ethnic and immigrant workers (Hondagneu-Sotelo 1997). While white women's entrepreneurship takes place largely in the formal economy, Latina women entrepreneurs are more active in the informal economy than their white counterparts. This is especially true for immigrant women. More often than white women, Latinas work as independent contractors in the informal economy, selling their labor "under the table" to meet their own economic and social needs.

Latina women, especially immigrants from Mexico, have a long history of working in informal sector jobs in the U.S. Southwest (Romero 1992; Ruiz 1987). New labor demands in the informal U.S. economy, created by processes of economic restructuring, continue to be met by immigrant workers. Pierrette Hondagneu-Sotelo (1997) contends that "high-income professionals and managers employed in advanced producer services have generated an entire "reorganization of the consumption structure," creating new labor demands in the informal sector for unique luxury goods, personal services, and residential and commercial gentrification" (p. 122). Immigrant women working in the informal economy fill many personal household and domestic services positions.

Hondagneu-Sotelo (1994) explores trends of paid domestic work among Mexican immigrant women and examines how work fosters permanent settlement for these women and their families in the United States. She argues that historically, domestic work has been an important institution through which immigrant women have become integrated into society. Most of the undocumented immigrant women in her study perform non-live-in domestic work. Because obtaining the first domestic job is difficult, many new immigrant women use family and friends to assist in finding employment or subcontract their services to well-established immigrant women with steady customers before building their own clientele. These women turn to immigrant social networks rather than Chicanos for assistance because cultural, social, and economic differences mitigate against the establishment of relationships between these two groups (Hondagneu-Sotelo 1994). The informal work culture of paid domestic workers allows immigrant women to build community ties and social relationships which can consolidate settlement.

In his study of undocumented immigrants, Leo Chavez (1992) details the benefits and drawbacks of domestic work for immigrant women. Advantages of domestic work include control over one's schedule, flexibility, and the ability to reconcile work and family demands. Despite such advantages, the domestic work performed by undocumented immigrant women is inherently volatile with wide variations in pay (Chavez 1992; Hondagneu-Sotelo 1994). Domestic workers also are vulnerable to work-related abuses like not being paid at all for their work (Chavez 1992). Some immigrant women supplement their income by combining domestic work with other jobs like vending or home-based day care for other immigrant women's children (Hondagneu-Sotelo 1994).

Immigrant women workers have been particularly numerous in Southern California's garment industry, which overall is characterized by instability, low wages, and lack of government supervision (Gomez-Quinones 1994). Homework and piecework have been increasing practices within this industry. Gomez-Quinones (1994) details some of the advantages of homework for immigrant women: doing as much work as one is able, keeping irregular hours, and working at home. But, due to lack of government supervision, these women workers often experience exploitative conditions.

> Cheating on wages occurred, as well as sudden reductions of wages for the same work. Flexibility of work deluded workers into thinking their bosses were "friendly." Undocumented female children were often an extra source of labor in homework arrangements (Gomez-Quinones 1994:286).

These workers frequently have low wages, few fringe benefits, and experience violations of minimum wage and overtime standards. Further, some of these workers are not registered at any shop or work for shops that are not licensed by the state (Gomez-Quinones 1994).

In their study of Mexican and Cuban immigrant women homeworkers, M. Patricia Fernandez-Kelly and Anna Garcia (1989) find that Mexican and Cuban women in the United States seek garment homework as a way to reconcile responsibilities of family with wage earning. They suggest that differences in class background and household composition have led to contrasting experiences of Mexican and Cuban homeworkers. Mexican women homeworkers in Los Angeles, California, appear to be economically and politically vulnerable due to their poor or working class backgrounds and sometimes undocumented status. In their sample of Mexican women, Fernandez-Kelly and Garcia (1989) find a higher percentage of female-headed households which creates a need for women's employment. In contrast, the Cuban women homeworkers in Miami, Florida, came from more varied class backgrounds. Many of their husbands were able to tap into co-ethnic resources of the Cuban business community. Due to such economic strides, many Cuban women use industrial homework to supplement the household income while still attending to family concerns.

Some of the women entrepreneurs in my study also work at home in order to reconcile responsibilities of family with wage earning. But, a significant difference arises with respect to the control that industrial homeworkers and home-based business owners exert over their own labor. Industrial homework is contingent on negotiating wages, hours, and workload with an employer (Boris 1987; Fernandez-Kelly and Garcia 1989; Gomez-Quinones 1994). Business ownership allows women greater flexibility and control over work load, hours, payment, and choice of business clients and customers, but introduces greater risk because most small businesses fail within the first five years.

LATINA ENTREPRENEURSHIP IN THE U.S.

Table 5.3 Class of Worker, Hispanic and Non-Hispanic White Females Age 16 and Over, 1990

Class of Worker	Hispanic Women	Non-Hispanic White Women
Percentage Distribution		
Total Percent	100. 0	100. 0
(thousands)	(3 421)	(30 612)
Private Wage and Salary	80. 3	78. 6
Local Government	8. 3	8. 2
State Government	4. 4	5. 1
Federal Government	2. 8	2. 6
Self-Employed	3. 8	5. 1
Unpaid Family	. 4	. 5

Source: U.S. Bureau of the Census, 1993b.

Latina women have a history of entrepreneurship in the informal United States economy. This is particularly true of immigrant women, especially those who are new arrivals or undocumented. In recent years, there have been large proportionate increases in Latina self-employment rates in the formal economy too. We can speculate that those Latina women who establish businesses in the formal economy are, in large part, American-born or have migrated and permanently settled in the United States. Nationally, a lower proportion of Latina women are self-employed compared to white women (Table 5.3). However, the percentage of self-employed women who are of Hispanic origin nearly doubled from 1975 to 1990 in the United States (Devine 1994).

The number of Hispanic-owned businesses has significantly increased in the United States over the past decade. The U.S. Bureau of the Census (1996b) documents that from 1987 to 1992 Hispanic-owned firms increased 83 percent and their receipts increased 195 percent from $24.7 billion to $72.8 billion. Comparable data for all businesses show a 26 percent increase in number, while receipts grew 67 percent for the same time period (Bureau of the Census 1996b). About one-third of these Hispanic-owned firms are in California (Bureau of the Census 1996b).

Table 5.4 Distribution of All U.S. Firms and Hispanic-Owned Firms by Industrial Category, 1992.

	Hispanic-Owned Firms	All U.S. Firms
Total (Number)	771, 708	17, 253, 143
Percent	100. 0	100. 0
Industrial Category		
Construction	10. 6	12. 6
Manufacturing	3. 0	2. 4
Wholesale Trade	3. 1	2. 3
Retail Trade	14. 4	14. 0
Finance	11. 3	6. 4
Services	45. 1	45. 0
Not Classified	5. 1	6. 9

Source: U.S. Bureau of the Census, 1996b.

Like all firms in the United States, the majority of Hispanic-owned firms (45 percent) are concentrated in the service industries, and 51 percent of these Hispanic-owned service firms are in business and personal services (Bureau of the Census 1996b). Retail trade (14 percent) accounted for the next largest concentration of Hispanic-owned firms (Bureau of the Census 1996b).

Businesses owned by Latina women also have increased significantly. Data from the National Foundation for Women Business Owners suggests that between 1987 and 1996 the number of Hispanic women-owned firms in the United States increased by 206 percent, their employment grew by 487 percent, and their sales jumped by 534 percent (*San Diego Business Journal* 1997). Nationwide, most minority women-owned firms are in the service industry (56 percent) and a high proportion are in retail (19 percent) (*San Diego Business Journal* 1997).

In my study, this is also the case. Of the Latina women, over half own service businesses; one-third own retail ventures. Three Latinas own businesses in male-dominated industries: One owns a construction business (special trade contracting); another owns a manufacturing firm. In both these cases, their husbands are highly integrated in the day-to-day functioning of the business. Another Latina owns an electrical company with a male business partner.

There are numerous approaches to examining why ethnic minorities and immigrants form small scale business enterprises in the Unites States. Some studies place the entrepreneurship patterns of immigrant and ethnic groups within the larger economic system. The dual labor market model is a well-documented perspective that views the labor force in terms of two economic sectors: primary and secondary. In the primary sector, composed of large bureaucracies and relatively stable production and sales, there are high-status professional and managerial jobs and, in the lower tier, white-collar clerical or blue-collar skilled or semi-skilled work. The secondary sector is characterized by many small firms with low capital investment and unstable product demand. Jobs in this sector are defined by their poor working conditions, low wages, lack of advancement potential, and little job security. In this segmented labor market, immigrants and men and women of color are disproportionately in the secondary sector in the United States.

In his work on immigrant entrepreneurship, Don Mar (1991) describes another economic sector: the ethnic labor market in which ethnic entrepreneurs use ethnic labor. Mar's (1991) research on Chinese immigrant workers and Park's (1997) study of Koreans in New York find that workers in the ethnic labor market are generally paid lower wages and have less promotional opportunities than those in other labor market sectors. Such research suggests that the ethnic labor market represents a lower tier of the secondary market.

Portes and Bach (1985) emphasize the benefits for immigrant co-ethnic employees working in ethnic enclaves, labor market niches in which immigrants' culture and internal solidarity are preserved. In such enclaves, like the Cuban community in Miami, Florida, ethnic or immigrant businesses often rely on customers and workers of a common culture and background. It is suggested that ethnic enclaves act as economic buffer zones that shield members of the same ethnic group from larger market forces and allow the survival and possible upward mobility of new immigrants who might not know the host culture and language (Fernandez-Kelly and Garcia 1989; Portes and Bach 1985).

The ethnic enclave perspective does not apply to all immigrant groups. The extent to which ethnic enclaves act as vehicles for upward social mobility has been challenged (Mar 1991; Sanders and Nee 1987). The emphasis placed on co-ethnic customers and workers for business success has been questioned, as in the case of Korean business owners in New York (Park 1997). In his study of Tucson, Arizona's Hispanic business elite, David Torres (1990) argues that both mainstream and ethnic networks are important for Mexican American entrepreneurs in developing their businesses. Half of his sample used mainstream and ethnic networks, while the other half recognized the importance of penetrating the "white" network but stated that they could not do so; they relied on ethnic networks or sheer experience to develop their businesses (Torres 1990). Nonethnic networks are important to Mexican American entrepreneurs because they can be used to legitimate the business beyond the ethnic community, secure financial backing, and obtain skilled employees (Torres 1990).

Some scholars have developed a resource-based view of immigrant and ethnic entrepreneurship. Ivan Light and Edna Bonacich (1988) ask why immigrants in general, and Koreans in particular, are more frequently self-employed than other Americans. They argue that the older concept of middleman minorities is too narrow to describe the process of immigrant and ethnic entrepreneurship in the United States. The concept of middleman minorities has often been used to describe entrepreneurial ethnic minorities who cluster in commercial occupations in Third World countries, such as Jews of the diaspora, East Indians in Uganda, and religious minorities in India. Light and Bonacich (1988) argue that the theory of middleman minorities is too restrictive to apply to the United States because of its orientation toward Third World contexts, in which commercial roles are often disdained unlike the United States where entrepreneurs are cultural heroes.

Instead, they develop the concepts of class resources (bourgeoisie material assets, knowledge, and skills) and ethnic resources (social features of a group) used by entrepreneurs for business success. In the case of Koreans in Los Angeles, both ethnic and class resources enabled their entrepreneurship. Class resources of Korean immigrants include a high educational attainment, ample savings, and middle or upper-middle social class origins. Koreans also have substantial ethnic resources.

> Koreans passed business information among themselves; worked long hours; mobilized unpaid family labor; maintained expected patterns of nepotism and employer paternalism; praised a Calvinist deity; utilized alumni, family, and congregational solidarities; thought of themselves as sojourners; expressed satisfaction with poorly remunerated work; and utilized rotating credit associations in financing their businesses (Light and Bonacich 1988:19).

In an earlier study comparing entrepreneurship among Chinese, Japanese, and African Americans in the United States, Light (1972) specifies the importance of rotating credit associations for entrepreneurship. While the prewar Chinese and Japanese successfully developed small businesses by raising capital through rotating credit associations, African Americans who migrated to industrial cities did not form such associations and had a harder time raising capital. Light explains this difference in terms of group solidarity. Japanese and Chinese immigrants before World War II came from a few areas of their home countries and erected elaborate structures of organizations based on locale of emigration. In contrast, African Americans did not have the localized solidarity required to sustain such associations. They had lost touch with their African origins, had no opportunity during slavery to set up businesses, and did not particularly identify with their home areas in the South.

What is the role of women in ethnic- or immigrant-owned enterprises? There is a noticeable pattern of business ownership among immigrant men in the United States that is supported by family labor consisting of wives, parents, children, siblings, and other relatives (Light and Bonacich 1988; Park 1997). For instance, most Korean-owned businesses are initiated by men (Park 1997). Men usually register their businesses under their own name, but still often benefit from their wives' (often unpaid) labor in the business. "When immigrant men plan to open a business, Korean patriarchal ideology plays a role, and wives and other kin are expected to cooperate in whatever way they can. The business is directed by the male household head" (Park 1997:116). The economic contribution of women who work in family businesses is often taken for granted by husbands and wives. Those businesses initiated by Korean immigrant women are often in women-dominated industries like beauty and fashion.

ETHNIC SOLIDARITY AND LATINA ENTREPRENEURS

It appears that some immigrant and ethnic business owners might benefit from ethnic solidarity, but is this the case for Latina entrepreneurs in San Diego? I find that frameworks that emphasize ethnic solidarity for entrepreneurial success do not fit with the entrepreneurial experiences of the Latina women in this book. In fact, Latina women unanimously agree that ethnic support networks do not function to benefit their businesses.

Their comments included:

I don't get that much business from the Hispanic community. It's mostly business that is around the area of the shop.

Hispanics are not a very united group. I find Hispanics don't help one another.

I don't find solidarity with Hispanic people in business.

I don't feel part of the Hispanic community.

I'm a member of the Hispanic Chamber but it hasn't gotten me any business.

Recall Gloria Morales, the owner of a personnel agency which has two employees: an Asian American woman, who is the receptionist, and a Latino, who helps with personnel placement. Gloria elaborates on her experiences as a Latina business owner.

The Hispanic community is not very good about helping their own. The Asian is very, very good about helping their own and using their own companies and their own organizations that you go to, they will use them. But the Hispanic community, for some reason, and I have said this for years, they don't use their own. They don't really help each other and scratch each other's backs like some of the other groups do and I honestly don't know what's behind this. I find that is, they get to a point and it's everybody for themselves, and within the Hispanic Chamber, umm, they, as far as actually using their business, I think they're getting better and I think they realize it themselves and are trying to do it.

Gloria emphasizes that she has not generated business from organizations designed to develop connections between Hispanic business owners, like the Hispanic Chamber of Commerce.

Likewise, Elaine Rodriguez, owner of a computer consulting firm, has not generated business from the Hispanic organizational functions that she has attended. "I'll hand out cards and no one ever calls," Elaine explains. Elaine does not feel support from other Latino/a business owners or customers.

I find that other Latinos are not supportive. It's not about organization, it's about our culture. Our culture has a lot to learn. I'm not saying all are bad, but there are quite a few who don't want you to succeed. "If I'm down in the dumps, I want you there too." Most of my contacts have been through Anglos. It hasn't been Hispanic.

Elaine observes few Latinos in the computer consulting industry in San Diego, and even fewer Latinos use her services. It is interesting that class-related issues come up in Elaine's response. She refers to other Hispanics who are "down in the dumps" and unwilling to support her business. Elaine comes from a working class family in Texas where "the mayor was Hispanic, business people were Hispanic." But, from Elaine's perspective, many more Latinos in San Diego are low-payed workers, she characterizes as "fast food chain" workers, who have neither the money nor the desire to support her business.

Elaine's business currently does not have employees because, as Elaine puts it, they cost too much.

Eva Cruz agrees that there is little comaradrie or support from other Latinos. Eva has two Latino and three white employees in her catering business. "I don't see any special loyalty from Hispanic customers," Eva explains, "My customers come to me, and come back to me, because they are happy with me."

Other research also confirms that the entrepreneurial experiences of Latinos may differ significantly from Asians and other minorities who use group strategies to achieve entrepreneurial success. Focusing on immigrant and native-born self-employed persons of Mexican ancestry, David Torres (1988) finds that Chicanos are more successful than Mexican immigrants in nontraditional lines of business and that class resources are more important than ethnic resources (social features of the group) in predicting their increased income.

> While both Mexican immigrants and Mexican-Americans may benefit from the presence of Hispanic markets and some degree of ethnic cooperation, quantitative evidence implies that, with the acquisition of class resources, a discernible number of Mexican-American entrepreneurs are venturing out of protected markets into the mainstream economy (Torres 1990:39).

Torres' study in Tucson, Arizona indicates that there is a market niche sustained by the Mexican-ancestry community. But within this niche, ethnic resources are abundant while class resources are limited. Torres (1990) argues that even though this niche acts as an important nurturing ground for many entrepreneurs, "its limited class resources are not enough to retain these ambitious entrepreneurs who ultimately turn to mainstream class resources" (p. 46).

The Latinas in my study felt an unwillingness from other Latinos to support their businesses. This unwillingness may, in fact, result from a higher level of solidarity in the Latino working class community. Torres (1990) points out that Mexican-American entrepreneurs who have assimilated into the mainstream economy may be perceived in a negative light by those who identify strongly with the Mexican or Latin American culture. This makes it difficult for these entrepreneurs to optimize performance in any one sector: the mainstream or the ethnic niche. Even though he emphasizes the importance of class resources and nonethnic networks for Mexican American entrepreneurial success, Torres points out that ethnic networks may still be important in the formative years of some Hispanic businesses. Assistance by minority public sector officials and Hispanic social and business organizations also is important.

Torres focuses primarily on male entrepreneurs without considering the significant role of gender. Lack of solidarity felt by Latina women could relate, in part, to their gender. Three Latina women commented that some Hispanic business organizations were male-oriented or male-dominated. Construction company owner, Cynthia Valdes, suggests that Latina business women are particularly disadvantaged because of their ethnicity and gender. When discussing her relationships with other Latinos in business, she states, "There are many minority people in bureaucratic roles. I've had a lot of bad experiences with them. I don't find solidarity with Hispanic people in business. And being a woman they think you're a dummy." Cynthia's statement underscores the fact that her experiences as an entrepreneur are colored by her ethnic identity and gender. She continues, "So I don't find solidarity among Hispanic businesses. It might be different among men."

If Latina women aren't relying on ethnic social networks for their business success, where do they find clients and customers? Eva Cruz finds most of her customers through word-of-mouth endorsements or local phone book advertisements. These are typical avenues Latina women used for finding business. Nine other Latinas also relied heavily on phone book advertising to bring in initial customers and word-of-mouth endorsements. They were in industries such as retail trade (bookstore, copy center, and an electrical shop) and services, like temporary personnel help, translation, and musical services. Twelve Latina women used mainstream business connections from previous employment or professional associations to establish a customer base. These women owned businesses in high technology, construction, computer services, catalog sales, and publishing.

FAMILY AS SOCIAL CAPITAL

In contrast to studies that concentrate on common ethnicity as a source of social capital, I find that the family is an important institution that Latina women entrepreneurs draw on to succeed as business owners. In their study on immigrant self-employment, Sanders and Nee (1996) emphasize the importance of family in providing social capital that immigrants can draw on in their pursuit of economic advancement because families "involve the mutual obligation and trust characteristic of solidaristic small groups" (p. 233). The family can support self-employment by furnishing labor, enabling the pooling of financial resources, and economizing on production and transaction costs: informal subleasing arrangements in which homeowners share their residence with other family members can promote economic capital accumulation, intrafamily loans can facilitate new businesses, and relying on family labor reduces operating costs (Sanders and Nee 1996).

In Chapter 4, I considered the nature and impact of social capital for women entrepreneurs. Recall that most Latina women (55 percent) did not identify themselves as having a mentor, someone who they could go to regularly for advice or assistance with their businesses. Although none of the Latina women identified a family member as a mentor, they still underscored the significance of familial assistance in their businesses. A higher percentage of Latina than white women used family sources of economic capital for business start-up. The spouse is especially important to some of these Latina women. A higher proportion of Latina compared to white women are married. Of the 15 Latina women who are married, 47 percent characterize their husbands as highly integrated with business activities. This proportion is higher than the married white women, of whom only 23 percent state that their husbands were integrated. I argued in Chapter 4 that having a husband in the same industry increases the likelihood that a business partnership will form. Also, having adult children increases the chances. However, for some Latina women, viewing the labor market as devoid of other employment options also acts as a catalyst for business partnership between husbands and wives. This was the case for Silvia Carrillo and Heather Reyes, whose husbands joined their businesses after being laid off from previous employment.

While seven Latina women characterized their husbands as integrated in their businesses, two of these seven women described their businesses as sole proprietorships in their own name; two have legal partnerships with their husbands; and three have incorporated businesses, in which both are employees of the company.

In the cases where the business is a sole proprietorship in the woman's name, the husband works as an employee in the company. This is true of Silvia Carrillo's business, and I asked her if there was any benefit to having the business in her name only. "I haven't felt one way or the other," Silvia responds, "Being a minority business enterprise, jobs under a certain amount, they don't have to comply with minority outreach so they go to whoever they want." Silvia explains that the business remains in her name because she originally established the business, which her husband later joined. Despite her sole proprietor status, it is interesting that she still states, "Both my husband and I are equal in business."

In their study of immigrant entrepreneurs, Sanders and Nee (1996) argue that household composition impacts family-based social capital: The presence of spouses, related adults, and to a lesser degree teenagers, are potential sources of capital pooling and family labor. We know that some of the Latina women in this study relied on the economic capital of family members to establish their businesses, but to what extent might these Latina business women benefit from family labor?

If we take a closer look at Latina women who have employees, we find some evidence to suggest that they are using family labor, but not to the extent that immigrant small business owners use extended family members. Forty six percent of the Latina-owned businesses with employees use family labor (Table 5.5). But in each case that family employee is the woman's husband. A much lower proportion of white women with employees (19 percent) hired employees who were family members and, in each of these cases, the employee was the woman's husband. The other six Latina-owned businesses with employees used formal hiring channels, such as advertisements in newspapers or trade association publications, to hire employees unrelated to them.

Table 5.5 Profile of Employees of Latina- and White-Owned Businesses in My Study, 1997

Characteristic	Latina-Owned Businesses with Employees (N=11)	White-Owned Businesses with Employees (N=21)
Percentage Distribution		
Relationship to Employee		
Family Member Present	45. 5	19. 0
No Relation to Any Employee	54. 5	81. 0
Racial/Ethnic Background of Employee		
White Employees Only	0. 0	57. 1
Latino Employees Only	18. 2	0. 0
More than One Ethnicity among Employees	81. 8	42. 9

Further, I find little evidence to support the idea that these Latina women are capitalizing on co-ethnic labor. There were only two businesses in which all the employees were Latino. One is Silvia Carrillo's translation business, in which her Latino husband works as her employee; the other is Marie Lopez's publication business. Marie and her business partner have six employees, three male, three female. Because the publication targets the Latino community, Marie argues that it was important to establish a bilingual staff with connections to the local Latino community and Mexico. "They are very supportive of the magazine," Marie says of her employees, "They really want to get it off the ground." Marie plans to increase the number of employees, but for now, is being cautious about expanding too quickly. The remaining nine Latina-owned businesses with employees have ethnically diverse workplaces, including predominantly white and Latino employees. One of these has mostly Latino employees (greater than 50 percent). Many of the businesses owned by the white women (43 percent) also have ethnically diverse workplaces; however, interestingly, a high proportion of these have only white employees (57 percent) and none have only Latino employees.

GENDER DISCRIMINATION, ETHNICITY, AND CULTURAL CAPITAL

Recent political rhetoric, which has fueled attacks on affirmative action policies, suggests that gender and ethnic discrimination are no longer salient issues in the workplace and educational arena. We know from a number of sociological studies, however, that discrimination and prejudice still permeate the work force. This can be seen in the sexual harassment and disparagement of women workers (Rosenberg et al 1993; Swerdlow 1989) and in discriminatory hiring practices that exclude ethnic minorities, women, and inner city residents from jobs (England 1992; Kirschenman and Neckerman 1991; Wilson 1996).

I asked the Latina women their impressions of being a minority woman in business. What forms of discrimination have they encountered as entrepreneurs, and how do they respond to such prejudice? As detailed in Chapter 4, gender prejudice and discrimination affects women entrepreneurs' experiences in business. Eight Latina women emphasized incidents involving gender over ethnic discrimination as most significant in potentially closing doors of business opportunity as entrepreneurs.

Marie Lopez argues that for her, gender discrimination appears to be an issue south of the border. "When dealing with clients, my partner [who is male] does most of the networking in Mexico. Most of the storeowners are men, and respond better to my partner. We have the magazine in some store fronts in TJ [Tijiuna, Mexico]," states Marie. Marie finds obvious benefits of being Hispanic because she runs a publication that targets the Latino community.

Claudia Sanchez has had the experience of people assuming that her husband is the sole business owner: "I could tell you hundreds and thousands of stories. I mean people walk in here or walk up to us and presume that I'm the secretary and he's the engineer. Daily. Everyday it happens." Likewise, Cynthia Valdes, who has a business partnership in construction with her husband, finds this to be the case.

> I could tell you stories that would raise the hair on your head. We were in a meeting to negotiate for extra work, everyone knew we were married and in business together, except for one guy who said to us, "I know why you are here," to my husband, "Why are you here?" pointing to me. I get that a lot. I get people who assume I don't know anything about the job.

Gloria Morales also has encountered gender prejudice and discrimination. She describes a typical occurrence at a Chamber of Commerce event:

> John [my husband] and I will stand side by side at a Chamber function and someone will say, "So John, what does your company do?" You'll see them

immediately respond, these are other men especially, immediately respond to him because he's a male and they assume that we are joint owners of the company and they will talk to him before they talk to me. He'll say, "Well, she's the boss, she's the owner, you have to talk to her about that..." I think that men are more comfortable with other men and I think they would prefer to work with a man and are still interested in mostly male-owned companies.

Sensing that men prefer to work with other men and that they still characterize women in support roles, these women feel disadvantaged as women business owners. However, Gloria also emphasizes one important benefit of being a minority woman entrepreneur: "I probably do have an advantage over a white male sex company of the same kind I do, only because there are still some companies that have affirmative action in place and are willing to give someone a chance." As long as policies exist to counter the gender prejudice she has felt at business functions, Gloria believes that she will at least have a chance to continue to build her business. Eva Cruz, party planner and caterer, and Vicki Torres, electrical company owner, also state that their minority business status has enabled them to secure more work than they would have been able to secure without affirmative action policies.

Four Latina women emphasized ethnic over gender discrimination as most significant in potentially closing doors of business opportunity. Elaine Rodriguez established her computer consulting business in 1992. Elaine has encountered ethnic prejudice within this industry and strategically attempts to hide her ethnicity for this reason. When she first opened her business, she made initial client contacts over the phone. "When I first started my business, what I would say is, "This is Elaine from CompuTech." I never used my last name. I didn't want doors of opportunity to close for me because of a name." Elaine underscores her need to prove herself, her ability to be a good business woman, but felt she wouldn't be given that opportunity due to ethnic prejudice and discrimination. When starting her company, Elaine wouldn't give her last name over the phone because she didn't want people to identify her as Hispanic and possibly lose business because of customers' ethnic biases.

While Elaine hides her last name from potential business clients, Nora Ortiz, public relations firm owner, talks of her advantage of not looking "too Hispanic."

There is a great deal of suspicion of minorities. I know that there is still discrimination out there, but I have brown eyes and I'm blond and I don't have an accent, so I don't look Mexican in San Diego. . . . I have told some people that I'm Hispanic and they say, "You don't look Hispanic."

Elaine and Nora argue that they can further their business activities and goals by not acknowledging their ethnic identity—by not sounding or looking "Hispanic." From these stories, it appears that cultural capital in business is related to ethnic identity. Those who are viewed as Anglo have greater capital than those labeled "Hispanic" in mainstream business settings. Denise Segura (1986) argues that because of the pervasiveness of racism, Chicanos are usually consigned to unskilled or semiskilled labor and not typically viewed as professionals. She argues that such a labeling process is detrimental to all Chicanos. Suzanne Oboler (1995) finds that Latin American immigrants are critical of the fact that Hispanics are differentiated from whites in the U.S. They perceive the term Hispanic as a term of segregation of "us" from the mainstream that signifies discrimination against Latinos. Entrepreneur Loretta Paredes agrees. Loretta argues that there is too much emphasis on groups and divisions between people in the United States. Loretta argues, "To classify people is bad. I raised my kids to respect other people. I think the biggest separator of people is the government" because it divides Americans into different classifications.

Some Latina women attempt to avoid ethnic classifications like Hispanic by not revealing characteristics about themselves that might place them in this category. We can characterize this response as the outcome of what Bourdieu (1977) calls symbolic violence, the imposition of systems of symbolism and meaning that determine and support relations of domination. Language is used to produce certain categories of understanding which support existing social hierarchies. Symbolic violence is a mode of domination in which those who don't have the means of speech view themselves in the discourse of "those who are legitimate authorities and who can name and represent" (Mahar et al 1990:14). Some Latina women entrepreneurs recognize the power of the category Hispanic and reject this label when identifying themselves in the mainstream business community.

CONCLUSION

In the two decades after 1970, Latinas rapidly increased their labor market participation, while still clustering in technical, sales, administrative support, and services positions. Latinas in the United States continue to have lower median incomes compared to white women, and their families have significantly higher poverty rates. Over the past 20 years, there has been an increase in higher income Latino households. The number of Latino households with incomes of $50,000 or higher (1988 dollars) in the United States increased 234 percent between 1972 and 1988. Still, those with incomes of less than $25,000 represented 56 percent of Latino households in 1990, but only 46 percent of non-Latino households (Rochin and de la Torre, 1996).

The group of Latina women in my study are more affluent than most other Latino families in the United States. They have grown up in working- or middle-class homes, have at least a high school diploma, and have been able to accumulate the forms of capital necessary to establish a business. But, not all the women were encouraged to become active labor force participants when growing up.

Most of the sixties generation women were prompted by their parents to learn basic secretarial skills as a back up plan in case of financial emergency. In contrast, women from the Reagan era were encouraged by their parents to pursue advanced degrees and professional or managerial positions in the labor market. Adelaida Del Castillo (1996) has argued that we should understand that Chicano and Mexican gendered behavior in families is more variable and complex than traditionally conceived. Drawing on field research and studies from the 1970s and 1980s, Del Castillo contends that these families should not be characterized generally as male dominated, nor based on rigid gender roles that privilege traditional patriarchal domestic arrangements. I find that gendered behavior and expectations were varied among the families of the Latina women as they grew up, especially across generations of these women.

Latina women entrepreneurs are among a growing number of minority women business owners. I sought to analyze more closely these women's patterns of entrepreneurship by drawing on the immigrant and ethnic entrepreneurship literature. Frameworks emphasizing ethnic solidarity for entrepreneurial success do not fit with the experiences of the Latinas in my study. In contrast to studies that concentrate on common ethnicity as a source of social capital, I find that the family is an important institution used by Latina women. A higher percentage of Latina than white women used family sources of economic capital for business start-up. Proportionally, more Latina women characterize their husbands as integrated with business activities too. Some of these women use family labor, but in all cases that family member is their husband. Further, little evidence supports the fact that these Latina women capitalize on co-ethnic labor; only two businesses employed Latinos only and most employed white and Latino workers. Eight Latina women emphasized gender discrimination as most significant in potentially closing doors of business opportunity. Four Latinas focused on incidents involving ethnic discrimination.

CHAPTER 6

Conclusions: The Meaning of Entrepreneurship

The entrepreneurial endeavors of the women in this book have developed within the United States labor market and its capitalistic economy. In his classic work, *The Protestant Ethic and the Spirit of Capitalism*, Max Weber (1904–05/1958) underscores the importance of the Protestant ethos for generating a new economic ethic, the spirit of capitalism, that shaped the nature of Western capitalism. Weber's vision of capitalism and entrepreneurship is grounded in the advance of rationality. For Weber, capitalism is an economically rational system, linked to the Protestant ethic and complemented by the principles of frugality and accounting for money. It is a system of calculating and instrumentally rational actors who desire to make money for its own sake.

In their eight-year study of an entrepreneurial family in Mexico, Larissa Lomnitz and Marisol Perez Lizaur (1982) find a different vision of entrepreneurship. For the Gomez family entrepreneurs, hard work and profit merit recognition if such material rewards solidify personal bonds and the care of dependents.

> Money is valuable insofar as it brings prestige to self and family; prestige is achieved by generosity, lifestyle and also by being a good entrepreneur. If an aunt is ill one will spend a whole morning at the hospital; taking care of relations is more important than time at work. Business is done whenever the opportunity arises; this gives the activity an "adventurous" unsystematic quality. The same applies to the use of capital; travel, presents, and good living often take precedence over investments, while frugality may be seen as "stinginess." (Lomnitz and Lizaur 1982:36).

In their case study, Lomnitz and Lizaur (1982) describe a group of entrepreneurs who gain rewards by using their businesses to solidify personal bonds, uphold their lifestyles and engage in generosity, rather than by emphasizing profit for profit's sake.

I find a similar vision of entrepreneurship among the white and Latina women entrepreneurs in this book. In my face-to-face interviews, I asked the women about the major advantages of business ownership. Several women (about 10 percent) emphasized the unlimited amount of money one can make as an entrepreneur. "You can make as much money as you're capable," states Anita Jordan. But most of the other women cherished the autonomy of entrepreneurship over profit. In fact, some could be making more money as waged or salaried employees, perhaps the more rational choice. But, these women choose to make less, while gaining freedom, flexibility, and control. Lee-Gosselin's and Grise's study (1990), in which they asked women entrepreneurs about their major satisfactions and frustrations in business, also finds that many women value the sense of self accomplishment (22 percent), autonomy, and independence (21 percent) achieved through business ownership.

Margot James elaborates on the flexibility that business ownership has brought her.

> One of the reasons I enjoy what I do is the flexibility. I have other interests besides paid work. I do a lot of volunteer community work. . . . I have decided that whatever needs I have, I could sacrifice some level of income for flexibility. I made that conscious decision.

Cynthia Valdes argues that part of the reason she established a home-based business was for the flexibility it would offer with a family.

> Once you get used to the lifestyle, it's hard to imagine not having a flexible schedule. We have always been more concerned with money and flexibility than security. We work a lot with people with security in mind. They can't conceive of the risk you take. For us, the house is the insurance against the jobs we take. We are always on the line. There's a kind of excitement to it. It's like playing the lottery. You have to be extremely determined to stick with it and want the independent lifestyle. . . . But I think that some people don't have the spirit to stick with the risk.

For women with young children, having a home-based business allows them to reconcile working for pay with taking care of household and child care responsibilities. Samantha Hatch emphasizes that she has control over her work schedule and hours. A divorced parent of two school-age children, Samantha shares custody with her ex-husband. "I can control my hours. When I'm with them [my children], I'm with them. When I'm not, I can work time and a half and I could not do that in any other situation," Samantha explains. When she was married, Samantha spent years working as a salaried employee, and as a mother and a wife, before owning her business. She describes that time in her life.

> Before I was running all the time. I could never get a break, and you just burn out like that. You can't do it, you know? Super women are the ones now that are moving up to the mountains and leaving their families and leaving their jobs and saying, "Screw that." You know? They're saying, "I have breast cancer and I don't want to do this anymore. You've sucked the life out of me, or I've allowed you to."

For Samantha, owning a business has meant more control over her schedule. Likewise, Jayne Kanter finds that, rather than going out and schmoozing for additional business at social functions, "I'd rather come home and play with my kids. And I do." As the principle in her architecture firm, Jayne has the freedom to decide how many clients she wants and what ways to get them.

In business for less than two years, Jody Wood has found that building her business has meant long hours, longer than the typical 40-hour work week. But she hopes that once she has an established clientele, she'll have more flexibility for a family too.

Opening a business also has meant longer work hours for Claudia Sanchez. But she still values the control she has by being a business owner.

> I mean once and a while I'll just get rubbed the wrong way really badly [with clients or vendors] and I'll just invite the person to leave or just terminate the phone call because they're being just a little too much. It's a huge advantage, being a business owner. . . . I can set the philosophy of this company and the philosophy is nobody has to put up with abuse. We don't have to be abusive in return or rude. In fact, we will be polite and respond appropriately in all cases, but we don't have to put up with it. And we don't. And I'm proud of that.

Laura O'Neil also elaborates on this benefit of being able to choose with whom you work.

> I can cultivate the people that I actually enjoyed working with and I don't have to call on the "idiots," or if I go out on a sales call and I find that this is going to be difficult or if I'm getting the feeling that he's or she's going to be difficult, I don't have to do it. No, you know, I just weigh it out. I say, well, if it's only a

month's profits, maybe I can come up with it. If it's going to be long term, do I really want to have this person in my face a couple of times a week?

WHERE DO THEY GO FROM HERE?

What are the goals of these women entrepreneurs for the future? What do they want from their businesses, and how do these goals relate to their own social needs and economic objectives? I asked the women if they would elaborate on any plans they might have for business growth, like hiring employees or increasing revenues.

Table 6.1 Goals for the Future of the Women in My Study, 1997

Future Goal	Women in my sample (N=89)
Percentage distribution	
Business Growth	46. 1
No Business Growth	42. 7
Sell the Business	11. 2

About half of the women in my study expressed a desire for business growth. A large portion of these women (19 of the 41) wanted to grow their businesses by hiring employees and increasing the workload. Michelle Allen, owner of a public relations firm, wants to hire an employee in the future. "Because my business is young and because it's cyclical, it's hard to determine when work is needed. I would like to see it grow," states Michelle. Keri Slater's high technology business currently employs one person, in addition to Keri and her business partner. She hopes that in the future as many as one hundred employees will be doing software for them. Keri elaborates, "We have started a consulting company and we are developing products on the side. The last company I was a partner in, we had grown to over 300 employees."

Increasing the number of clients and projects without hiring employees was another growth strategy stated by many of these women. Fifteen women stated that while they wanted to increase revenues, they didn't want to achieve this by hiring (in some cases, more) employees. Shelley Johnson elaborates on her decision to grow her marketing consulting business without employees. She argues that growing the company is always something on her mind, but she has recently been entertaining different growth options.

I've come to a fork in the road. One path leads to, well if this business is going to grow into a successful business, successfully financially as well as how your peers see it, at some point I've thought about perhaps moving into an agency, a marketing group. The other path is to finish taking the current course, interacting with more clients per month, but this path won't take me as far as the other. My gut intuition is telling me to do this. I will recognize when I reach that peak. This is what I'm capable of bringing in, top out at that and see if that's enough. The other road, becoming part of an agency, has more status and prestige, but more problems, dealing with employees.

Shelley explains that for most of her career, she has done sales and management, been responsible for employees, and had to deal with their work and personal problems. Since 1995, Shelley has owned her business without employees. Shelley states, "And I ask myself, 'Is it something I really want? Do I want to go through that again?'"

Lastly, six women, all in services, collaborated with other industry experts as a growth strategy. Among these are Dina Berst, Jill Copeland, and Samantha Hatch. Dina, owner of a health care consulting business, finds that other health care specialists, including therapists and medical doctors, have recently expressed an interest in working with her, which would increase her client base. Psychotherapist Jill Copeland plans to expand her business by training other therapists and speaking at workshops. Samantha Hatch also finds that collaborating with other industry experts is the most practical way for her business to grow. Samantha started collaborating with other people two years ago.

I will go after a larger contract, but I will bid with another person or I will bring them in with me. I have a subcontractor right now on something. In fact, we talked about going into a partnership and I was seriously looking at that over the last year as a way of generating more revenue, stabilizing the work load and just that synergy for another person and having that stability as opposed to every contract having a different group.

Samantha finds that establishing rapport with other business owners in the same industry, and going after contracts together, allows her to increase revenues without expanding her business through employees.

Thirty eight women in my study (43 percent) did not have plans for growth. Among these, sixteen women emphasized that, in order for their business to grow, they would need to hire employees, which represents a hassle and bother that they don't want. Employees also can signal a lack of control that many of these women are not willing to relinquish.

Kay Martin, owner of a health and beauty services business, states, "I want a simple life. I don't want to be bothered with employees, withholding taxes and all that. I do this from my heart, not to get rich." Lori Brown states that she doesn't want employees because she wants to keep her training services business simple. Likewise, real estate appraiser Doris Lamont argues, "We have decided not to have employees because then you have to supervise people. We didn't want that. We don't want the hassle."

Gail Mayfield, owner of a landscape architecture firm since 1984, finds that "A lot of times when firms get big, the partners are like figure heads. But we do our own project management and have qualified people. I like being hands on. I'm not sure that we'll get much bigger for this reason." Vicki Sanchez, owner of an electrical company, agrees, "At one point we had gotten up to 60 people [employees] but that's very tough because you lose control if you aren't prepared to handle that number of personnel. We are at 20 now, and that is a good size." Photography studio owner Pat Stevens also states, "We don't plan to hire employees. We like to keep tight control over things." Interior designer Andi Costello explains, "I've chosen not to have employees. It restricts growth but, I prefer not to have that kind of responsibility."

For all these women, more growth does not necessarily equal success in their eyes. Their success comes from managing small, yet profitable businesses that allow them to exert greater personal control. My findings are consistent with Lee-Gosselin's and Grise's study (1990) in which they find that many of their female respondents chose to maintain a small company to "preserve their own quality of life, to keep close contact with their employees and clients, and mostly, to stay close to operations" (p 432). While some women entrepreneurs pursued growth, most value small organization: "Small and very small stable business is "good and real business" for them" (Lee-Gosselin and Grise 1990:432).

Eight women in my study stated that they did not want business growth because of their age. Seventy-year-old, graphic designer Betty Simon argues, "I definitely do not want growth. . . . I'm 70 years old. I need the money and it's fun. It keeps me mentally alert and on top but I don't want to grow." Celia Robles, also in her 70s, agrees, "I do this to pay the bills and stay a float" largely because "Social Security doesn't cut it." Four other women, all in their mid-50s, view their business as something to do while looking forward to retirement. When I asked Silvia Carrillo, owner of a translation business, what plans she might have for growing her business she responded, "We ask ourselves that. We ask what we want to be doing, and we are just looking toward retirement."

Eva Cruz also explains,

> I don't want growth. No growth! I'm too old. I don't want any more money. I
> want security . . . . I go once a month and see my grandson in Arizona. At this

point in my life, I don't have ambition. Money isn't everything, and I think a lot of people in my age group are going through this.

For Eva, her success as a business owner comes from running a business that offers her security, while still allowing her time to spend with family and friends.

Four other women clearly specified that they did not want business growth because they have home-based businesses, designed to offer supplemental income while allowing them to take care of young children. This is the case with Katie Menard.

> I haven't thought of plans for the future or growth. I do this for some extra income and my little ones [children]. My husband wants to open an office elsewhere when they are grown, but now I like to be able to support the business and house.

While growth might be a possibility in the distant future, Katie has no such immediate plans. Katie explains that she spends about 40 hours per week on her secretarial business in addition to the time she takes on domestic responsibilities. "It's good to have a business at home because you can deal with the house things. And my kids have also gone out to clients' offices with me."

Ten women, five Latina and five white, specifically mentioned selling their existing businesses at some point in the future. This is the case with Rita Moore, owner of a bakery since the late 1970s. Rita, age 58, is ready to start relinquishing some of her business responsibilities.

> Within the next five years, I'll probably sell a portion of my business to an employee who was age 18 when we started. He's now 38. I want it to become an employee-owned business, but still come in and do the paperwork. I'd like them to take over the business. It's almost time to start powering down.

For Rita, powering down means handing over more of the business to her employees, one of whom has remained with the business since opening 20 years ago.

Sixty-one-year-old Maureen Davis also plans to sell the clientele from her beauty and massage business in the next few years.

> I'm planning to go into network marketing. I use a lot of essential oils in my business. Network marketing is where it's at. I mean, this working for $50 an hour is great if you're working. If you don't have a client, you're not getting $50. As far as my business, it's doing great, but I'm looking for a change. I'd

like to be out of here because there's so much going on out there. I want to do it
before I'm too old. I'm already old. I don't want to be old and poor. You can't
stop being old, but I certainly don't want to be old and poor.

Like Rita, Maureen is looking toward retirement, but is frightened by the
prospect of being "old and poor." Her strategy is to sell her existing business,
and begin working for an aromatherapy oil company that will allow her to profit
from her sales and the sales of other persons who she urges to join.

Gloria Morales, age 42, is also thinking over the possibility of selling her
business. She is frequently contacted by other firms interested in buying her
personnel services company.

> I don't know if I want to open another branch because that's really complicated.
> Perhaps there might be a time when I would, but actually at this point, I am
> working on a goal of mine that in three to five years, sell. I get a lot of offers
> from companies who like what my figures look like just because I am
> independent. It seems that every day I get an offer, a letter saying they are
> representing a company who is interested in acquiring a company or an
> independent company in San Diego, and so, hopefully there will be a market if
> I do decide to sell.

Gloria emphasizes that her original goal when she started her business was
to make enough to get her son through college. Her son is currently enrolled in
college, and once he graduates, Gloria will make more concrete plans for her
business' future.

It has always been Claudia Sanchez's plan to eventually sell her
manufacturing business. She and her husband have talked about what would
happen if the business was sold. "I'd actually look for another employment
opportunity outside the company. Ricardo would be the most needed because
he's the manufacturing side," Claudia states. For Claudia, selling the business
would likely mean that she would continue paid employment with another firm,
while her husband would oversee manufacturing of the newly merged business.

CONCLUSIONS AND NEW LINES OF RESEARCH

This study adds to the literature on gender and entrepreneurship in a number of
significant ways. Rather than grouping women together in a uniform category
and comparing women's and men's entrepreneurship, this study acknowledges
variations between women entrepreneurs based on race, ethnicity, and class
backgrounds. I have shown throughout this study how entrepreneurship is
colored by these significant differences. Women's pathways to business
ownership and uses of economic, social, and cultural capital vary when we take

such variables into account. I compare the entrepreneurial experiences of white and Latina women because this approach makes a significant contribution to the literature. These two groups are the most numerous among women entrepreneurs in San Diego County.

While accounting for the significance of gender, ethnicity, and class, I have explored the various pathways that women take to becoming entrepreneurs. I find five main reasons why women become small capitalists. The most cited reason was responding to family-related concerns, such as starting a home-based business to have flexibility with young children, establishing a partnership with a family member, or beginning a business after a divorce. Domestic arrangements have an important impact on these women's entrances into the labor force and affect their pathways to entrepreneurship. For some of the women, production in the home, in the form of a home-based business, allowed them to contribute to the family income while attending to domestic activities. In many of these cases, these women's work loads actually increased as they attempted to maintain profitable businesses and meet the needs of their family. A large portion of the women also established businesses because of desire for freedom from bureaucratic, iron cage work environments. Other pathways included being laid off, reacting to gender discrimination at work, and having the right timing and opportunity. Latinas were more likely than white women to establish businesses due to family-related concerns or after having been laid off.

Economic capital, resources that are directly convertible into money, is crucial for entrepreneurship. Most women used their own personal savings or credit as their primary source when starting their businesses. A higher percentage of white than Latina women used such personal resources. About 11 percent of my sample primarily turned to family members outside their immediate household for start-up capital. A higher percentage of Latina than white women used family sources. As children growing up, these women tended to be involved in productive activities that contributed somehow to the family income—Vicki Torres sold novelties or fireworks with her brothers and sisters and Cindy Kelley assisted her mother's photography business. This relationship of production shared by children and parents prompted the women to feel they could turn to family for economic assistance and their families knew they could trust them based on experience. Very few women turned to formal lending institutions for start-up capital. All these women were married at the time of starting their businesses, which tend to be atypical of most women-owned businesses. They all have employees, gross revenues well over $100,000 annually, and have always existed outside the home.

The class character of entrepreneurship becomes apparent when examining the typical sources of entrepreneurial economic capital: Personal finances, relatives with enough disposable income to invest, or a formal business loan.

Lack of access to these sources means the likelihood of establishing a business in the U.S. formal economy is severely curtailed. All of the women but five identified themselves as middle class. Having resources of the middle class is crucial for turning a business dream into reality in the United States. Further exploration of entrepreneurship should include analysis of gender and social class. Economically disadvantaged women are rarely able to pursue even modest dreams of business ownership because of limited opportunities and restricted financial resources (Rodriguez 1995).

What programs might assist low-income Americans in becoming entrepreneurs themselves? Grameen-style programs have sprung up throughout the United States since the mid 1980s, offering training, technical advice, and financial assistance in the form of loans. Knowing that poor people are generally shut out of business ownership in the formal economy, Muhammed Yunus founded the Grameen Bank in Bangladesh in 1983. The Bank gives micro loans to the poor to assist them in establishing their own businesses (based on skills most had or could easily develop) and requires borrowers to form groups to discuss each other's businesses. Grameen's 1,079 branches throughout the world have provided 2.1 million loans, mainly to rural women (Wright 1997). For poor women who gain assistance through such programs, what is the nature and size of their businesses? These loans appear to be enough to sustain micro-enterprises, or very small businesses, but to what extent might they allow for larger business ventures?

In addition to economic capital, social capital also proves crucial for entrepreneurial success. In this study, I equate strong-tie business relationships with the concept of mentoring, defined as having a trusted counselor or advisor in business. I asked the women if there were any people who they considered to be mentors whose advice or assistance they relied on during their time as a business owner. Almost half of the women did not characterize themselves as having a mentor in business. Of those with a mentor, 55 percent identified mentors from within their industry. A small number of women with mentors (23 percent) view family members as business mentors. These women all turned to family members, such as parents, who had experience as entrepreneurs themselves. My study finds that women entrepreneurs primarily rely on mentors who are men or both men and women mentors. Few named only other women as sources of mentorship.

Although a small portion of women entrepreneurs view other family members as business mentors, family still provides an important source of social capital. These women entrepreneurs do not enter the labor market as isolated individuals, but rather as members of family networks. Parents and siblings are often sources of advice, assistance, or financial support. Spouses often act as much needed social capital. Many women in my study were married. Unlike single or divorced women, married women lived in nuclear families and contributed to the household income with their spouses. In numerous cases, husband's income provided crucial financial support during business start-up.

One third of these married women (one fifth of the total sample) own a business in which their husband is regularly involved. A higher portion of married Latina compared to married white women characterize their husbands as highly integrated with business activities (47 and 23 percent, respectively). For both Latina and white women, having a husband in the same industry increases the likelihood that a business partnership will form. But, for some Latina women, viewing the labor market as devoid of other options also acted as a catalyst to business partnership between husbands and wives. It is interesting that women with dependent children were least likely to have their business activities integrated with their husband. Future studies on women's entrepreneurship should continue to assess the impact that domestic arrangements and household composition have on women's business ownership.

This study also focuses on cultural capital, which includes institutionalized, embodied, and objectified forms (Bourdieu 1986). One aspect of institutionalized cultural capital is educational qualifications. The women entrepreneurs in my study have a relatively high degree of schooling. All had at least a high school degree. More Latina than white women earned a high school diploma only, and a lower percentage of Latina than white women earned graduate degrees. Some industries are closed to entrepreneurs without advanced educational credentials. But many more fields don't have such professional gatekeeping. The women in these fields view advanced education as a way to primarily gain greater credibility. A college diploma has a legitimizing effect in business. For two women in my study, pretending to have college degrees opened up doors that led them to entrepreneurship in sales. Many of the women don't apply the knowledge they learned in school to their businesses. Most view networking and communication skills gained through work experience as most crucial to gaining respect as an entrepreneur.

How significant is embodied cultural capital as it relates to women entrepreneurs' dispositions, mannerisms, and tastes? I specifically focused on the women entrepreneurs who owned businesses in nontraditional industries in which they are one of the relatively few women entrepreneurs. How do these women use the cultural capital of dispositions and mannerisms to their benefit? They emphasize the importance of friendliness, kindness, and being good-natured in order to win over male peers, colleagues, and clients. Even though I find that the women in male-dominated industries play the careerist game by being complicit in some sexually offensive circumstances, these women use the power of business ownership to limit or avoid contact with those colleagues or clients who display such behavior.

Cultural capital is perhaps the most elusive form of capital to study. How does a researcher assess or measure mannerisms, dispositions, and tastes? I asked the women directly about how they gain respect as an entrepreneur. I asked, "What does acting professional mean to you? In other words, how might a business owner in this industry gain the confidence of clients or customers?" The women described their behavior in various business situations—some in which they wanted to impress a client or customer; others in which they responded to sexist commentary of male colleagues. For the women who I met face-to-face, I had the added benefit of seeing how they dressed, articulated themselves, and acted in the work place. But, in order to thoroughly study cultural capital, a researcher must be emerged in the setting through participant observation. Watching and listening to an entrepreneur in the business environment would enable a more in-depth exploration of the dynamics of cultural capital at work.

Before concluding this discussion of cultural capital, I want to revisit Bourdieu's definition and examine how ethnicity relates to cultural capital. Bourdieu's definition of cultural capital includes: the embodied state of dispositions, mannerisms, and tastes; the institutionalized state, involving educational qualifications and training; and the objectified state in the form of cultural goods (Bourdieu 1986). Our access to cultural capital relates to our position within the gender, race, and class hierarchies. For instance, ethnic and racial minorities have lower cultural capital in the form of educational attainment in the U.S. than white Americans. But doesn't ethnicity itself act as a form of cultural capital? By virtue of having an advanced degree, an individual has greater distinction in business than others. Isn't this also the case with racial and ethnic identity in business? In ethnic enclaves, ethnic and immigrant business owners can capitalize on shared ethnicity to promote the success of their businesses (Portes and Bach 1985). In mainstream business environments, racism and ethnic prejudice still exist that impact hiring and promotional practices and channel people of color into lower occupational positions (Collins 1989; Higginbotham 1994).

How does ethnicity as cultural capital impact the success of Latina entrepreneurs? The Latina women in this book all own and operate businesses in the mainstream business community of the formal economy. Some Latina women emphasize that their ethnic identity has closed doors of business opportunity for them. Elaine Rodriguez has encountered ethnic prejudice in the computer industry and attempts to strategically hide her ethnicity for this reason. With mostly all-white clientele, Elaine wouldn't give her last name over the phone because she didn't want people to identify her as Hispanic and possibly lose business due to clients' ethnic biases. Nora Ortiz talked of her advantage of not looking "too Hispanic" in the public relations field. From these stories, it appears that cultural capital in business is related to ethnic identity. Those who are viewed as white have greater capital than those labeled Hispanic when operating industries with predominantly white clients. Some Latina women attempt to avoid this ethnic label by not revealing characteristics about themselves that might place them in this category. They reject the label Hispanic when identifying themselves in the mainstream business community because they want to avoid potentially discriminatory practices.

I devoted one chapter entirely to Latina entrepreneurs because I wanted to use their entrepreneurial experiences to respond to the immigrant and ethnic entrepreneurship literature. Analyses emphasizing ethnic solidarity for entrepreneurial success do not fit with the experiences of the Latina women in this study. In contrast to research that concentrates on common ethnicity as a source of social capital, I find that the family is an important institution used by Latina entrepreneurs. As I have mentioned, a higher percentage of Latina than white women used family sources of economic capital for business start-up. Proportionally, more Latina women characterize their husbands as integrated with business activities too. Further, little evidence supports the fact that Latina women capitalize on co-ethnic labor; most employed white and Latino workers.

Much of the literature on Latina business ventures in the United States has focused on their activities in the informal economy. These can be particularly important sources of income for immigrants from Mexico and Latin America. But we should not focus on such informal activities while overlooking the thousands of Latina women who are establishing businesses within the formal U.S. economy. More work needs to assess the entrepreneurial experiences of these women and highlight differences between American-born and immigrant Latinas as business owners in the formal economy. I expect that results regarding Latina entrepreneurship will vary regionally within the United States. An important line of research would be to conduct studies on Latina-owned businesses in other areas of the country too. Examination of businesses that cross the U.S.-Mexico border would also be fruitful. Two women in this study have businesses that operate in the United States and Mexico. Eva Cruz caters social events on both sides of the border. Marie Lopez's publication is sold in both countries. It would be beneficial to develop studies that focus on differences between the Mexican and U.S. labor markets by examining women-owned businesses in Northern Mexico and Chicana- or Mexicana-owned businesses in the United States.

FINAL THOUGHTS

Women entrepreneurs maintain varying levels of economic, social, and cultural capital and strategically use these different forms of capital in their pathways to entrepreneurship. Their location in the social landscape determines their access to and accumulation of capital. Privileged economically, most of the women entrepreneurs in this book viewed themselves as middle class and were able to finance their own business ventures. Sometimes disadvantaged by gender or ethnic prejudice, these women entrepreneurs, nevertheless, acted strategically within the confines of the business world to keep their enterprises alive.

Economic success as an entrepreneur can be difficult to achieve. Often business owners' lives are filled with hard work, long hours, stress, and uncertainty. Many entrepreneurial ventures in the United States fail. But, women entrepreneurs feel they have more to gain through ownership than as employees. Perhaps they don't have the same amount of success measured in dollars, but, in their minds, success is also about having control over their work schedule and having freedom to choose with whom they work. For many women business owners, these obvious psychological and social benefits of being an entrepreneur outweigh the economic.

When I spoke with entrepreneur Rachel Maxwell, owner of a yoga business, she emphasized these social benefits and expressed her loyalty to other small business owners. She states that, even though large grocery stores and warehouse clubs are cheaper, she still patronizes her local corner market as much as possible.

> I've become much more aware of how I spend my money. I'm more conscious of say, like going over by this little market, it's an Iranian market. I'd like this market to stay in business. I'd like them still to be there. Luckys is going to be there forever. Why don't I go in and buy my cheese from the market and give them the business? It's who you're giving your business to. And I start going out of my way to give it to people who I want to support.

Since becoming a business owner in 1996, Rachel is more aware of supporting those who she wants to succeed in business. Even though the corner market can't compete with the prices of franchised grocery stores, Rachel argues that it's important to keep the smaller stores in business. Perhaps she feels empathy, being a business owner herself; or perhaps her willingness to support this store comes from a sense of nostalgia or longing for the way things used to be—a time when Mom and Pop stores frequented the neighborhood, when people knew their neighbors, and watched out for each other's children. In many ways these kinds of businesses have a special place in American history.

But, we are now in a time dominated by big business and franchisement. C. Wright Mills (1951) saw this in the 1950s: "This is no society of small entrepreneurs...above them is the big money; below them, the alienated employee...behind them, their world" (p. 59). George Ritzer and David Walczak (1986) further argue, "One gets the feeling that such small proprietorships are fighting a losing, rear-guard action against the irreversible trend toward larger size, greater efficiency, and more impersonality" (p. 290). But, the women in this book, and the millions of other entrepreneurs throughout the nation, continue to act against the prevailing tide of big business. Foregoing jobs in large corporations, these enterprising women establish their own small ventures in hopes of capturing some of the freedom, flexibility, and control that is missing from the contemporary American workplace.

Notes

Chapter 1 First Encounters

1. The names of my interviewees and some details regarding their backgrounds have been changed to protect their identities.

2. One of the best measures of self-employment in the United States comes from the Current Population Survey, in which delineations are made between wage and salary employment, self-employment, and unpaid family work. The designation self-employed worker includes a wide variety of persons: those who own sole proprietorships or partnerships and those who bring in miscellaneous income due to activities such as contracting their services or acting as independent sales representatives for other businesses. Self-employment data exclude entrepreneurs who have established incorporated businesses (thereby designated wage and salary workers).

Chapter 4 Capital and Entrepreneurship: Incorporating Gender and Ethnicity

1. Loans from the U.S. Small Business Administration (SBA) and federal procurement contracts for women-owned businesses have been made available. Through the Women's Business Ownership Act of 1988, long-term training, counseling, and networking centers were established for women business owners. In addition, the SBA has established a pilot program in which it prequalifies a loan guarantee for a woman business owner before she goes to a bank. In 1995, Wells Fargo Bank also launched a women's loan program. Despite such avenues of lending assistance, the women in my study still spoke of difficulties in securing loans due to factors like their short length of time in business or perceived gender discrimination.

2. It was unclear to me whether the loan officers contacted by Anita Jordon and Dawn Nelson were male or female.

3. I obtained fee information on several all-women's business organizations in San Diego County. Fees range considerably for various functions. In 1998, the U.S. Small Business Administration (SBA) offered all-women networking meetings once a month priced at $15 per meeting. Topics for 1998 included: networking, marketing, protecting business assets, violence in the workplace, investments, and business growth strategies. The SBA also offers business management seminars ranging from $5 to $95. Some of the sessions are free. Some women's networking groups have sessions designed to assist women in juggling personal and business concerns. A flyer advertising a Valentine Special networking meeting in February 1998 reads: "Girlfriend. . . . Is the only support you get coming from your Maidenform? . . . Owning a business can kill relationships. Learn how to make money and make every day Valentine's Day! . . . A self-professed "bad employee" and entrepreneur . . . reveals how love and money are powerful partners in keeping the fires alive in your relationships and your business." Other all-women's groups, such as Leads Clubs, involve weekly meetings geared toward business referrals. Leads Club membership fees for 1998 include an initial membership fee of $75 per year plus $25 per month.

4. Some feminists argue that women do indeed exhibit distinct differences from men, such as a more relational style of management (Helgesen 1990, Rosener 1990) and courtroom litigation (Menkel-Meadow 1985; Pierce 1995). Works emphasizing gender difference have been critiqued, however, for constructing male and female in terms of fundamental and binary oppositions, and inadvertently offering justification for continued gender inequities by widening the divide between "the rational male and the emotional female" (Marshall 1995; Swan 1994).

References

Aldrich, Howard E. 1989. "Networking Among Women Entrepreneurs." Pp. 103–132 in *Women Owned Businesses*, edited by O. Hagan, C. Rivchun, and D. Sexton. New York: Praeger.

Aldrich, Howard E., Amanda Brickman Elam, and Pat Ray Reese. 1995. "Strong Ties, Weak Ties, and Strangers: Do Women Owners Differ from Men in Their Use of Networking to Obtain Assistance?" *Working Paper #4*. Boston, MA: Small Business Foundation of America.

Aldrich, Howard E., Pat Ray Reese, and P. Dubini. 1989. "Women on the Verge of a Breakthrough? Networking among Entrepreneurs in the United States and Italy." *Entrepreneurship and Regional Development* 1:339–356.

Aldrich, Howard and Tomoaki Sakano. 1998. "Unbroken Ties." In *Networks, Markets, and the Pacific Rim*, edited by M. Fruin. New York: Oxford University Press.

Anderson, Margaret L. 1988. *Thinking about Women: Sociological Perspectives on Sex and Gender*. New York: MacMillan Publishing Company.

Baca Zinn, Maxine. 1989. "Family, Race, and Poverty in the Eighties." *Signs* 14:856–874.

–––. 1991. "Chicano Men and Masculinity." Pp. 221–232 in *The Sociology of Gender*, edited by L. Kramer. New York: St. Martin's Press.

Bechhofer, Frank, Brian Elliott, Monica Rushforth, and Richard Bland. 1974. "The Petits Bourgeois in the Class Structure: The Case of the Small Shopkeepers." Pp. 103–128 in *The Social Analysis of Class Structure*, edited by F. Parkin. London: Tavistock Publications.

Becker, Gary. 1975. *Human Capital: A Theoretical and Empirical Analysis*. New York: Columbia University Press.

–––. 1985. "Human Capital, Effort, and the Sexual Division of Labor." *Journal of Labor Economics* 3(suppl):533–558.

Beechey, Veronica. 1978. "Women and Production: A Critical Analysis of Some Sociological Theories of Women's Work." Pp. 155–197 in *Feminism and Materialism*, edited by A. Kuhn and A. Wolpe. London: Routledge and Kegan Paul.

Beeghley, Leonard. 1996. *The Structure of Social Stratification in the United States*. Boston, MA: Allyn and Bacon.

Bender, Henry. 1978. *Report on Women Business Owners*. New York: American Management Association.

Bird, Caroline. 1976. *Enterprising Women*. New York: Norton.

Blau, Francine. 1984. "Occupational Segregation and Labor Market Discrimination." Pp. 117–143 in *Sex Segregation in the Workplace: Trends, Explanations, Remedies*, edited by B. Reskin. Washington, DC: National Academy Press.

Blau, Francine and Anne Winkler. 1989. "Women in the Labor Force: An Overview." Pp. 265–286 in *Women: A Feminist Perspective*, edited by J. Freeman. Palo Alto, CA: Mayfield.

Bluestone, Barry and Bennett Harrison. 1982. *The Deindustrialization of America*. New York: Basic Books.

Boisjoly, Johanne, Greg Duncan, and Sandra Hofferth. 1995. "Access to Social Capital." *Journal of Family Issues* 16:609–631.

Bonacich, Edna. 1987. ""Making It" in America: A Social Evaluation of the Ethic of Immigrant Entrepreneurship." *Sociological Perspectives* 30:446–466.

— — —. 1993. "Asian and Latino Immigrants in the Los Angeles Garment Industry: An Exploration of the Relationship between Capitalism and Racial Oppression." Pp. 51–73 in *Immigration and Entrepreneurship: Culture, Capital, and Ethnic Networks*, edited by I. Light and P. Bhachu. New Brunswick, NJ: Transaction Publishers.

Boris, Eileen. 1987. "Homework and Women's Rights: The Case of the Vermont Kniters, 1980–1985." *Signs* 13:98–120.

Bourdieu, Pierre. 1977. *Outline of a Theory of Practice*. London: Cambridge University Press.

— — —. 1984. *Distinction: A Social Critique of the Judgement of Taste*. Cambridge, MA: Harvard University Press.

— — —. 1986. "The Forms of Capital." Pp. 241–258 in *Handbook of Theory and Research for the Sociology of Education*, edited by J. Richardson. New York: Greenwood Press.

— — —. 1989. "Social Space and Symbolic Power." *Sociological Theory* 7:14–25.

Bourdieu, Pierre and Jean-Claude Passeron. 1977. *Reproduction in Education, Society, and Culture*. London: Sage Publications.

Bregger, John E. 1996. "Measuring Self-Employment in the United States." *Monthly Labor Review* Jan/Feb:3–9.

Brush, Candida. 1992. "Research on Women Business Owners: Past Trends, A New Perspective and Future Directions." *Entrepreneurship: Theory and Practice* 16:5–30.

Carr, Deborah. 1996. "Two Paths to Self-Employment? Women's and Men's Self-Employment in the United States, 1980." *Work and Occupations* 23:26–53.

Carter, Deborah and Reginald Wilson. 1993. *Eleventh Annual Status Report on Minorities in Higher Education*. Washington DC: American Council on Education.

Chavez, Leo. 1992. *Shadowed Lives: Undocumented Immigrants in American Society*. Fort Worth, TX: Harcourt Brace Publishers.

Chavez, Leo, F. Allan Hubbell, Shiraz Mishra, and R. Burciaga Valdez. 1997. "Undocumented Latina Immigrants in Orange County, California: A Comparative Analysis." *International Migration Review* 1:88–107.

Chinoy, Ely. 1955. *Automobile Workers and the American Dream*. New York: Doubleday.

Christensen, Kathleen. 1987. "Women and Home-Based Work." *Social Policy* 15:54–57.

———. 1988. *Women and Homebased Work: The Unspoken Contract*. New York: Henry Holt and Company.

Chodorow, Nancy. 1979. "Mothering, Male Dominance, and Capitalism." Pp. 83–106 in *Capitalist Patriarchy and the Case for Socialist Feminism*, edited by Z. Eisenstein. New York: Monthly Review Press.

Chow, Esther Ngan-ling. 1994. "Asian American Women at Work: Survival, Resistance, and Coping." Pp. 203–227 in *Women of Color in U.S. Society*, edited by M. Baca Zinn and B. Thornton Dill. Philadelphia: Temple University Press.

Coleman, James. 1988. "Social Capital in the Creation of Human Capital." *American Journal of Sociology* 94(suppl):S95–S120.

Collins, Sharon. 1989. "The Marginalization of Black Executives." *Social Problems* 36:317–331.

Dallalfar, Arlene. 1994. "Iranian Women as Immigrant Entrepreneurs." *Gender & Society* 8:541–561.

Davies-Netzley, Sally. 1998. "Women above the Glass Ceiling: Perceptions on Corporate Mobility and Strategies for Success." *Gender & Society* 12:339–355.

Del Castillo, Adelaida. 1996. "Gender and Its Discontinuities in Male/Female Domestic Relations: Mexicans in Cross-Cultural Context." Pp. 207–230 in *Chicanas/Chicanos at the Crossroads: Social, Economic, and Political Change*, edited by D. Maciel and I. Ortiz. Tucson: The University of Arizona Press.

Den Uyl, Marion. 1995. *Invisible Barriers: Gender, Caste, and Kinship in a Southern Indian Village*. Utrecht, The Netherlands: International Books.

Devine, Theresa J. 1994. "Characteristics of Self-Employed Women in the United States." *Monthly Labor Review* Mar:20–34.

Dunn, Dana, editor. 1997. *Workplace/Women's Place: An Anthology*. Los Angeles, CA: Roxbury Publishing Company.

Dye, Thomas. 1995. *Who's Running America? The Clinton Years*. Englewood Cliffs, NJ: Prentice Hall.

Ebert, Teresa. 1996. *Ludic Feminism and After: Postmodernism, Desire, and Labor in Late Capitalism*. Ann Arbor, MI: The University of Michigan Press.

Eisenstein, Zellah R. 1979. "Developing a Theory of Capitalist Patriarchy and Socialist Feminism." Pp. 5–40 in *Capitalist Patriarchy and the Case for Socialist Feminism*, edited by Z. Eisenstein. New York: Monthly Review Press.

Eitzen, D. Stanley and Maxine Baca Zinn, editors. 1989. *The Reshaping of America: Social Consequences of the Changing Economy*. Englewood Cliffs, NJ: Prentice Hall.

England, Paula. 1992. *Comparable Worth: Theories and Evidence*. New York: Aldine de Gruyter.

Fagenson, Ellen. 1993. "Personal Value Systems of Men and Women Entrepreneurs Versus Managers." *Journal of Business Venturing* 8:409–430.

Fernandez-Kelly, M. Patricia. 1994. "Towanda's Triumph: Social and Cultural Capital in the Transition to Adulthood in the Urban Ghetto." *International Journal of Urban Affairs* 18:88–111.

Fernandez-Kelly, M. Patricia and Anna Garcia. 1989. "Hispanic Women and Homework." Pp. 165–179 in *Homework: Historical and Contemporary Perspectives on Paid Labor at Home*, edited by E. Boris and C. Daniels. Urbana: The University of Illinois Press.

Gerson, Kathleen. 1985. *Hard Choices: How Women Decide about Work, Career, and Motherhood*. Berkeley: University of California Press.

Glenn, Evelyn Nakano. 1986. *Issei, Nisei, Warbride: Three Generations of Japanese American Women in Domestic Service*. Philadelphia: Temple University Press.

———. 1994. "Social Constructions of Mothering: A Thematic Overview." Pp. 1–29 in *Mothering: Ideology, Experience, and Agency*, edited by E. Nakano Glenn, G. Chang, and L. Forcey. New York: Routledge.

Goffee, Robert and Richard Scase. 1985. *Women in Charge: The Experience of Female Entrepreneurs*. London: George Allen & Unwin.

Gomez-Quinones, Juan. 1994. *Mexican American Labor, 1790–1990*. Albuquerque, NM: University of New Mexico Press.

Granfield, Robert and Thomas Koenig. 1992. "Pathways into Elite Law Firms: Professional Stratification and Social Networks." *Research in Politics and Society* 4:325–351.

Granovetter, Mark. 1985. "The Strength of Weak Ties." *American Journal of Sociology* 78:1360–1380.

Gregg, Gail. 1985. "Women Entrepreneurs: The Second Generation." *Across the Board* 22:10–18.

Hagan, John, Marjorie Zatz, Bruce Arnold, and Fiona Kay. 1991. "Cultural Capital, Gender, and the Structural Transformation of Legal Practice." *Law & Society Review* 25:239–262.

Hartmann, Heidi. 1979. "Capitalism, Patriarchy, and Job Segregation by Sex." *Signs* 1:137–169.

———. 1981. "The Unhappy Marriage of Marxism and Feminism: Towards a Progressive Union." Pp. 1–41 in *Women and Revolution*, edited by L. Sargent. Boston, MA: South End Press.

Hays, William and Charles Mindel. 1973. "Extended Kinship Relations in Black and White Families." *Journal of Marriage and the Family* 35:51–57.

Helgesen, Sally. 1990. *The Female Advantage: Women's Ways of Leadership*. Des Plaines, IL: Doubleday.

Herz, D. E. and B. H. Wootton. 1996. "Women in the Workforce: An Overview." Pp. 44–78 in *The American Woman, 1996–1997: Where We Stand*, edited by C. Costello and B. Kivimac Krimgold. New York: Norton.

Higginbotham, Elizabeth. 1994. "Black Professional Women: Job Ceilings and Employment." Pp. 113–131 in *Women of Color in U.S. Society*, edited by M. Baca Zinn and B. Thornton Dill. Philadelphia: Temple University Press.

Hisrich, Robert. 1989. "Women Entrepreneurs: Problems and Prescriptions for Success in the Future." Pp. 3–32 in *Women-Owned Businesses*, edited by O. Hagan, C. Rivchun, and D. Sexton. New York: Praeger.

Hisrich, Robert and Marie O'Brien. 1981. "The Woman Entrepreneur from a Business and Sociological Perspective." Pp. 21–39 in *Frontiers of Entrepreneurial Research: Proceedings of the 1981 Conference on Entrepreneurship*. Wellesley, MA: Babson College.

Hisrich, Robert and Candida Brush. 1984. "The Woman Entrepreneur: Management Skills and Business Problems." *Journal of Small Business Management* 22:30–37.

Hochschild, Arlie Russel. 1989. *The Second Shift: Working Parents and the Revolution at Home*. New York: Viking.

Hondagneu-Sotelo, Pierrette. 1994. *Gendered Transitions: Mexican Experiences of Immigration*. Berkeley: University of California Press.

———. 1997. "The History of Mexican Undocumented Settlement in the United States." Pp. 115–134 in *Challenging Fronteras: Structuring Latina and Latino Lives in the U.S.*, edited by M. Romero, P. Hondagneu-Sotelo, and V. Ortiz. New York: Routledge.

Jackall, Robert. 1988. *Moral Mazes: The World of Corporate Managers*. New York:Oxford University Press.

Jenssen, Svenn and Lars Kolvereid. 1992. "The Entrepreneurs' Reasons Leading to Start-up as Determinants of Survival and Failure among Norweigian New Ventures." Pp. 120–133 in *International Perspectives on Entrepreneurship Research*, edited by S. Birley and I.C. MacMillan. New York: North-Holland.

Jones, Jacqueline. 1985. *Labor of Love, Labor of Sorrow: Black Women, Work, and the Family from Slavery to the Present*. New York: Basic Books.

Kanter, Rosabeth Moss. 1977. *Men and Women of the Corporation*. New York: Basic Books.

Kirschenman, Joleen and Kathryn Neckerman. 1991. "Hiring Strategies, Racial Bias, and Inner-City Workers." *Social Problems* 38:433–447.

Kozol, Jonathan. 1991. *Savage Inequalities: Children in America's Schools*. New York: Harper Perennial.

Lavoie, Dina. 1984/1985. "A New Era for Female Entrepreneurship in the 80s." *Journal of Small Business, Canada* (winter):34–43.

Lee-Gosselin, Helene and Jacques Grise. 1990. "Are Women Owner-Managers Challenging Our Definitions of Entrepreneurship? An Indepth Survey." *Journal of Business Ethics* 9:423–433.

Light, Ivan. 1972. *Ethnic Enterprise in America: Business and Welfare Among Chinese, Japanese, and Blacks*. Berkeley: University of California Press.

Light, Ivan and Edna Bonacich. 1988. *Immigrant Entrepreneurs: Koreans in Los Angeles 1965–1982*. Berkeley: University of California Press.

Lomnitz, Larissa and Marisol Perez Lizaur. 1982. "Culture and Ideology Among Mexican Entrepreneurs." Pp. 23–43 in *Culture and Ideology: Anthropological Perspectives*, edited by J. R. Barstow. Minneapolis: Minnesota Latin American Series.

Loscocco, Karyn and Joyce Robinson. 1991. "Barriers to Small Business Success among Women." *Gender and Society* 5:511–532.

Mahar, Cheleen, Richard Harker, and Chris Wilkes. 1990. "The Basic Theoretical Position." Pp. 1–25 in *An Introduction to the Work of Pierre Bourdieu: The Practice of Theory*, edited by R. Harker, C. Mahar, and C. Wilkes. New York: St Martin's Press.

Mar, Don. 1991. "Another Look at the Enclave Economy Thesis: Chinese Immigrants in the Ethnic Labor Market." *Amerasia Journal* 17:5–21.

Marlow, Sue and Adam Strange. 1994. "Female Entrepreneurs - Success by Whose Standards?" Pp. 172–184 in *Women in Management: A Developing Presence*, edited by M. Tanton. London: Routledge.

Marshall, Judi. 1995. *Women Managers Moving On: Exploring Career and Life Choices*. London: Routledge.

Martin, Linda. 1994. "Power, Continuity, and Change: Decoding Black and White Women Managers" Experience in Local Government." Pp. 110–140 in *Women in Management: A Developing Presence*, edited by M. Tanton. London: Routledge.

Menkel-Meadow, Carrie. 1985. "Portia in a Different Voice: Speculations on a Women's Lawyering Process." *Berkeley Women's Law Journal* Fall:39–63.

Mills, C. Wright. 1951. *White Collar: The American Middle Classes*. New York: Oxford University Press.

Mincer, Jacob and Solomon Polachek. 1978. "Women's Earnings Reexamined." *Journal of Human Resources* 13:118–134.

Mirande, Alfredo and Evangelina Enriquez. 1979. *La Chicana: The Mexican American Woman*. Chicago: University of Chicago Press.

Mitchell, Juliet. 1998. "The Position of Women." Pp. 173–191 in *Social Class and Stratification: Classic Statements and Theoretical Debates*, edited by R. Levine. Lanham, MD: Rowman & Littlefield.

Moore, Dorothy and E. Holly Buttner. 1997. *Women Entrepreneurs: Moving Beyond the Glass Ceiling*. Thousand Oaks, CA: Sage.

Moore, Gwen. 1988. "Women in Elite Positions: Insiders or Outsiders?" *Sociological Forum* 3:566–585.

Neider, Linda. 1987. "A Preliminary Investigation of Female Entrepreneurs in Florida." *Journal of Small Business Management* 25:22–29.

Newman, Katherine. 1988. *Falling From Grace: The Experience of Downward Mobility in the American Middle Class*. New York: The Free Press.

———. 1993. *Declining Fortunes: The Withering of the American Dream*. New York: Basic Books.

Oboler, Suzanne. 1995. *Ethnic Labels, Latino Lives: Identity and the Politics of (Re)Presentation in the United States*. Minneapolis: University of Minnesota.

Office of Public Affairs. 1993. *Fact Finder 1992–93. County of San Diego*. San Diego: Office of Public Affairs.

Ortiz, Vilma. 1994. "Women of Color: A Demographic Overview." Pp. 13–40 in *Women of Color in U.S. Society*, edited by Maxine Baca Zinn and Bonnie Thornton Dill. Philadelphia: Temple University Press.

Ortiz, Vilma, and Rosemary Santana-Cooney. 1984. "Sex Role Attitudes and Labor Force Participation among Young Hispanic Females and Non-Hispanic White Females." *Social Science Quarterly* 65:392–400.

Park, Kyeyoung. 1997. *The Korean American Dream: Immigrants and Small Business in New York City*. Ithaca, NY: Cornell University Press.

Parsons, Talcott, and Neil Smelser. 1956. *Economy and Society: A Study in the Integration of Economic and Social Theory*. Glencoe: Free Press.

Pedraza, Silvia. 1991. "Women and Migration: The Social Consequences of Gender." *Annual Reviews of Sociology* 17:303–325.

Pellegrino, Eric T. and Barry L. Reece. 1982. "Perceived Formative and Operational Problems Encountered by Female Entrepreneurs in Retail and Service Firms." *Journal of Small Business Management* 20:15–24.

Pierce, Jennifer. 1995. *Gender Trials: Emotional Lives in Contemporary Law Firms*. Berkeley: University of California Press.

Polakow, Valerie. 1993. *Lives on the Edge: Single Mothers and their Children in the Other America*. Chicago: The University of Chicago Press.

Portes, Alejandro and Robert Bach. 1985. *Latin Journey: Cuban and Mexican Immigrants in the United States*. Berkeley: University of California Press.

Portes, Alejandro and Cynthia Truelove. 1987. "Making Sense of Diversity: Recent Research on Hispanic Minorities in the United States." *Annual Review of Sociology* 13:359–385.

Rapp, Rayna. 1982. "Family and Class in Contemporary America." Pp. 168–187 in *Rethinking the Family*, edited by B. Thorne and M. Yalom. New York: Longman.

Reese, Pat Ray. 1993. "Resource Acquisition: Does Gender Make a Difference?" Pp 441–458 in *Entrepreneurship Research: Global Perspectives*, edited by S. Birley and I. C. MacMillan. New York: North-Holland.

Reskin, Barbara. 1993. "Sex Segregation in the Workplace." *Annual Review of Sociology* 19:241–270.

Ritzer, George and David Walczak. 1986. *Working: Conflict and Change*. Engelwood Cliffs, NJ: Prentice Hall.

Rochin, Refugio and Adela de la Torre. 1996. "Chicanas/os in the Economy: Issues and Challenges Since 1970." Pp. 52–80 in *Chicanas/Chicanos at the Crossroads: Social, Economic, and Political Change*, edited by D. Maciel and I. Ortiz. Tucson: The University of Arizona Press.

Rodriguez, Cheryl. 1995. *Women, Microenterprises, and the Politics of Self-Help*. New York: Garland Publishing.

Rogers, Barbara. 1980. *The Domestication of Women: Discrimination in Developing Societies*. London: Tavistock.

Romero, Mary. 1992. *Maid in the USA*. New York: Routledge.

– – –. 1997. "Introduction." Pp. xiii-xix in *Challenging Fronteras: Structuring Latina and Latino Lives in the U.S.*, edited by M. Romero, P. Hondagneu-Sotelo, and V. Ortiz. New York: Routledge.

Roschelle, Anne. 1997. *No More Kin: Exploring Race, Class, and Gender in Family Networks*. Thousand Oaks, CA: Sage.

Rosenberg, Janet, Harry Perlstadt, and William Phillips. 1993. "Now That We Are Here: Discrimination, Disparagement and Harassment at Work and the Experience of Women Lawyers," *Gender & Society* 7:415–433.

Rosener, Judy. 1990. "Ways Women Lead." *Harvard Business Review* 68(Nov/Dec):119–125.

– – –. 1995. *America's Competitive Secret: Utilizing Women as a Management Strategy*. New York: Oxford University Press.

Rubin, Lillian. 1994. *Families on the Fault Line: America's Working Class Speaks about the Family, the Economy, Race, and Ethnicity*. New York: HarperPerennial.

Ruiz, Vicki L. 1987. "By the Day or the Week: Mexicana Domestic Workers in El Paso." Pp. 61–76 in *Women on the U.S.-Mexico Border: Responses to Change*, edited by V. Ruiz and S. Tiano. Boston: Allen and Unwin.

Safa, Helen I. 1981. "Runaway Shops and Female Employment: The Search for Cheap Labor." *Signs* 7:418–433.

San Diego Business Journal. 1997. "Eight Million Firms in U.S. are Women-Owned Businesses." 7 July, special report.

Sandag Info. 1997. "Regional Employment Inventory." Nov-Dec.

Sandag Info. 1998. "San Diego Regional Employment Clusters." May-June.

Sanders, Jimy and Victor Nee. 1987. "Limits of Ethnic Solidarity in the Ethnic Enclave Economy." *American Sociological Review* 54:809–820.

— — —. 1996. "Immigrant Self-Employment: The Family as Social Capital and the Value of Human Capital." *American Sociological Review* 61:231–249.

Scase, Richard and Robert Goffee. 1982. *The Entrepreneurial Middle Class.* London: Croom Helm.

Scheinberg, Stephen and Ian MacMillan. 1988. "An 11 County Study of Motivations to Start a Business." Pp. 669–687 in *Frontiers of Entrepreneurship Research*, edited by B. A. Kirchhoff, W. A. Long, W. E. McMillan, K. H. Vesper, and W. E. Wetzel. Wellesley, MA: Babson College.

Schumpeter, Joseph. 1934. *The Theory of Economic Development: An Inquiry into Profits, Capital, Interest, and the Business Cycle.* Cambridge: Harvard University Press.

Schwartz, Eleanor Brantley. 1976. "Entrepreneurship: A New Female Frontier." *Journal of Contemporary Business* 5:47–76.

Scott, Joan Norman. 1996. "Watching the Changes: Women in Law." Pp. 19–41 in *Women and Minorities in American Professions*, edited by J. Tang and E. Smith. New York: State University of New York Press.

Segura, Denise. 1986. "Chicanas and Triple Oppression in the Labor Force." Pp. 47– 65 in *Chicana Voices: Intersections of Class, Race, and Gender*, edited by T. Cordova, N. Cantu, G. Cardenas, J. Garcia, and C. Sierra. Austin TX: The Center for Mexican American Studies.

— — —. 1994. "Inside the Worlds of Chicana and Mexican Immigrant Women." Pp. 95–111 in *Women of Color in U.S. Society.* edited by M. Baca Zinn and B. Thornton Dill. Philadelphia: Temple University Press.

Shapero, Albert. 1975. "The Displaced, Uncomfortable Entrepreneur." *Psychology Today* 9:83–88.

Small Business Administration. 1995. *News Release on Census Data for Women- Owned Businesses.* Washington DC: Small Business Administration.

Spalter-Roth, Roberta M. 1988. "Vending on the Streets: City Policy, Gentrification, and Public Patriarchy." Pp. 272–294 in *Women and the Politics of Empowerment*, edited by A. Bookman and S. Morgen. Philadelphia: Temple University Press.

Staber, Udo and Howard Aldrich. 1995. "Cross-National Similarities in the Personal Networks of Small Business Owners: A Comparison of Two Regions in North America." *Canadian Journal of Sociology* 20:441–467.

Swan, Elaine. 1994. "Managing Emotion." Pp. 89–109 in *Women in Management: A Developing Presence*, edited by M. Tanton. London: Routledge.

Swerdlow, Marian. 1989. "Men's Accommodations to Women Entering a Nontraditional Occupation." *Gender & Society* 3:373–387.

Tang, Joyce and Earl Smith. 1996. "Introduction." Pp. 1–18 in *Women and Minorities in American Professions*, edited by J. Tang and E. Smith. New York: State University of New York Press.

Tiano, Susan. 1994. *Patriarchy on the Line: Labor, Gender, and Ideology in the Mexican Maquila Industry*. Philadelphia: Temple University Press.

Torres, David. 1988. "Success and the Mexican-American Businessperson." Pp. 313–334 in *Research in the Sociology of Organizations*, edited by S. Bacharach and N. DiTomaso. Greenwich, CT: JAI Press.

———. 1990. "Dynamics Behind the Formation of a Business Class: Tucson's Hispanic Business Elite." *Hispanic Journal of Behavioral Sciences* 12:25–49.

U.S. Bureau of the Census. 1976. *Women-Owned Businesses: 1972 Economic Census*. Washington, DC: GPO.

———. 1986. *Women-Owned Businesses: 1982 Economic Census*. Washington, DC: GPO.

———. 1991. "Summary." *Survey of Minority Owned Business Enterprises: 1987 Economic Census*. Washington, DC: GPO.

———. 1993a. "The Hispanic Population in the United States: March 1993." *Current Population Reports*. Series P20–475. Washington, DC: GPO.

———. 1993b. *Social and Economic Characteristics of the United States: 1990 Census of the Population*, Series CP-2-1. Washington, DC: GPO.

———. 1994. "Educational Attainment in the United States: March 1993 and 1992." *Current Population Reports*, Series P-20–476. Washington, DC: GPO.

———. 1995. *Statistical Abstract of the United States: 1995*. Washington, DC: GPO.

———. 1996a. *Women-Owned Businesses: 1992 Economic Census*. Washington, DC: GPO.

———. 1996b. *Survey of Minority-Owned Business Enterprises, Hispanic: 1992 Economic Census*. Washington, DC: GPO.

U.S. Department of Labor, Women's Bureau. 1996. "Twenty Facts on Women Workers." *Facts on Working Women*. Washington, DC: GPO.

U.S. Department of Labor, U.S. Bureau of Labor Statistics. 1995a. *Women in the Workforce: An Overview*. Washington, DC: GPO.

———. 1995b. *Employment and Earnings* 42(1). Washington, DC: GPO.

Van der Wees, Catherine and Henny Romijn. 1995. "Entrepreneurship and Small- and Microenterprise Development for Women: A Problematique in Search of Answers, a Policy in Search of Programs." Pp. 41–84 in *Women in Micro- and Small-Scale Enterprise Development*, edited by L. Dagnard and J. Havet. Boulder, CO: Westview Press.

Wagner, Roland and Diane Schaffer. 1980. "Social Networks and Survival Strategies: An Exploratory Study of Mexican American, Black, and Anglo Female Family Heads in

San Jose, California." Pp. 173–190 in *Twice a Minority: Mexican American Women*, edited by M. Melville. St Louis, MO: C. V. Mosby.

Waldinger, Roger. 1986. *Through the Eye of the Needle: Immigrants and Enterprise in New York's Garment Trades*. New York University Press.

Weber, Max. 1904–05/1958. *The Protestant Ethic and the Spirit of Capitalism*, translated by T. Parsons. New York: Charles Scribner's Sons.

— — —. 1946. *From Max Weber: Essays in Sociology*, edited by H. H. Gerth and C. W. Mills. New York: Oxford University Press.

— — —. 1968. *Economy and Society: An Outline of Interpretive Sociology*, edited by G. Roth and C. Wittich. New York: Bedminster Press.

Williams, Christine L. 1992. "The Glass Escalator: Hidden Advantages for Men in the "Female" Professions." *Social Problems* 39:253–267.

Wilson, William Julius. 1987. *The Truly Disadvantaged*. Chicago: University of Chicago Press.

— — —. 1996. *When Work Disappears: The World of the New Urban Poor*. New York: Vintage Books.

Wright, Robin. 1997. "Women as Engines Out of Poverty." *Los Angeles Times*, 27 May, section A, 1–6.

Wright, Rosemary. 1996. "Women in Computer Work: Controlled Progress in a Technical Occupation." Pp. 43–64 in *Women and Minorities in American Professions*, edited by J. Tang and E. Smith. New York: State University of New York Press.

Zavella, Patricia. 1984. *The Impact of the Sunbelt Industrialization on Chicanas*. Palo Alto, CA: Stanford University.

— — —. 1987. *Women's Work and Chicano Families: Cannery Workers of the Santa Clara Valley*. Ithaca, NY: Cornell University Press.

Zhou, Min. 1992. *Chinatown: The Socioeconomic Potential of an Urban Enclave*. Philadelphia: Temple University Press.

Zweigenhaft, Richard. 1987. "Minorities and Women of the Corporation: Will They Attain Seats of Power?" Pp. 37–62 in *Power Elites and Organizations*, edited by G. W. Domhoff and T. Dye. Newbury Park, CA: Sage Publications.

— — —. 1993. "Prep School and Public School Graduates of Harvard: A Longitudinal Study of the Accumulation of Social and Cultural Capital." *Journal of Higher Education* 64:211–225.

Name Index

Subject Index

affirmative action policies, 120

capital, *See* cultural capital; economic
capital; social capital
cultural capital:
definition of, 17, 82-83
and educational attainment, 83-84,
133
and ethnic discrimination, 120-121,
134-135
and gender bias, 91-95

deindustrialization, 48

economic capital:
definition of, 15-16, 61
family sources of, 5-6, 64-67
in the form of savings and credit, 62-
64
formal lending sources of, 67-70
entrepreneurship, *See* Hispanic-owned
businesses; home-based businesses;
immigrant and ethnic
entrepreneurship; Latina women in
this study;
self-employment; women-owned
firms;

women's entrepreneurship in this
study

glass ceiling, 10, 11, 53-54
Grameen Bank, 132

Hispanic-owned businesses:
nationwide:
number of, 110
by industry, 110
home-based businesses, 1-4, 35-39, 63,
103, 104, 109
124-125, 129, 131
human capital theories, 10, 83, 99-100

immigrant and ethnic entrepreneurship:
and class and ethnic resources, 14,
112-113, 115
ethnic enclaves, 14, 111-112
segmented labor market models, 14,
111

Latina women:
and business ownership nationwide,
110
and domestic work, 107-108
and educational attainment, 84, 98
and garment homework, 39, 108

www.ingramcontent.com/pod-product-compliance
Ingram Content Group UK Ltd.
Pitfield, Milton Keynes, MK11 3LW, UK
UKHW020429010325
455677UK00029B/1072